THE MOCK
OLYMPIAN

Michael Long

authorHOUSE®

AuthorHouse™ UK
1663 Liberty Drive
Bloomington, IN 47403 USA
www.authorhouse.co.uk
Phone: 0800.197.4150

Published by AuthorHouse 09/21/2016

ISBN: 978-1-5246-6288-2 (sc)
ISBN: 978-1-5246-6289-9 (hc)
ISBN: 978-1-5246-6287-5 (e)

Contents

Chapter 1.   The Idea..1

Chapter 2.   Athens – The Birthplace of the Marathon (and Me).....4

Chapter 3.   London – A Decathlon of Events 8

Chapter 4.   Tokyo – Please Let Me Run with You 16

Chapter 5.   Stockholm – Come Join the Joyride.......................21

Chapter 6.   Helsinki – The Beach Run 24

Chapter 7.   Istanbul – One Foot in Asia and One in Europe 27

Chapter 8.   Barcelona – The Run with All the *B*s ... Bad
Back, Blisters, and Bruises 29

Chapter 9.   Rome – The Run That Went Missing 33

Chapter 10. Paris – "Du Pain, Pas de Vin, du Boursin".............36

Chapter 11. Antwerp – The Diamond City................................40

Chapter 12. Berlin – Meet Her at the Love Parade 44

Chapter 13. Amsterdam – A Splash, No Hash.........................48

Chapter 14. Beijing – Lost in the Suburbs................................51

Chapter 15. Munich – Do I Risk a Beer? 58

Chapter 16. Montreal – Running with a Chilly Willy 63

Chapter 17. Moscow – From Russia with Pink Love 69

Chapter 18. Sydney – The City Versus the Beach.....................88

Chapter 19. Melbourne – The Best City on Earth.....................95

Chapter 20. Seoul – Back to the Marathon 100

Chapter 21. Los Angeles – A Run in the Happiest Place on
Earth...109

Chapter 22. Atlanta – I'm pregnant 118

Chapter 23. St. Louis – I Love Rock 'n' Roll............................125

Chapter 24. Mexico City – I Think You May Have a
             Drinking Problem 131
Chapter 25. Rio de Janeiro – In Search of the Showgirl 139

Epilogue: Was I Born to Run? 147
Summer Modern Olympic Games Chronology 153
My Olympic Tour Dates 155
The cast 157
Acknowledgements 159
About the Author 161
About the Book 163

It is the heartbeat, the very DNA of this organisation and a rallying cry for the athletes to come to the UK to perform at their very best and inspire the world.

—Sebastian Coe

Chapter 1

The Idea

July 2012
Islington, London

London was shaping up to host the 2012 Summer Olympic Games, and along with millions (although not all Londoners), I was excited to be able to live and experience the Olympics in my hometown. I had been behind London hosting the Olympics way back in 2004, when the bid was officially made. I had the "Back the Bid" sticker up in my living room window and had my entire team at work sign the online "Back the Bid" petition to do my bit to make sure the IOC (International Olympic Committee) knew London wanted the Olympics. On the day that London won the bid (6 July 2005), I watched the outcome live on TV in the reception of my office and was ecstatic. I was going on holiday the next day and what a way to start it.

Fast-forward to 2012. I had just had my thirty-second birthday. My friend Sarah had offered to host a little soiree to mark the occasion, which consisted of lots of her lovely homemade treats, wine, and good company. As Sarah gave me some presents, it was apparent that running was clearly something I was interested in. She gave me a headband with "Lovely Michael" embroidered on it, as well as *Time Out*'s complete guide to the history of the Olympics. A fantastic book, it covers each of the Summer Olympic Games in chronological order. As I sat on the sofa, I opened to page one, which showed the inaugural 1896 games held in Athens. A picture of the first Olympic stadium during the games was on the adjacent page. "That's where I finished my first marathon," I said to Sarah's boyfriend, James.

"With all the running you do, you have probably run in most of the cities that will follow," he replied.

I thought about it for a second and thought through the other runs, bike rides, and triathlons I had done previously. Sure, I had done Athens and various runs in London, but my other challenges outside the UK had been in Orlando, San Francisco, and Las Vegas; no other Olympic city featured. Food for thought.

The London 2012 Olympic Games came and by far exceeded my expectations. Living in a city hosting the games allowed me to experience the electric atmosphere on an hourly basis, and I was lucky enough to attend many of the events in Olympic Park itself. Sadly, though, the Olympics ended all too soon.

For the closing ceremony, my boyfriend, Steven, and I had decided to watch the games at one of my favourite haunts in Soho whilst enjoying dinner and a few cocktails, then staying over at a central London hotel. The last "show" of the Olympics did not disappoint, and for one last time, the entire bar threw itself into it and made the atmosphere fantastic. Singing, clapping, and laughing were in abundance. After all, this was a gay bar in Soho. The moment the Spice Girls appeared at the ceremony, I am certain it was not just me who screamed like a teenage girl. Now, I say this not knowing how much alcohol other tables had consumed; however, the bill for just Steven and me came to a whopping £244.97. If drinking were an Olympic sport, surely we would have been in with a chance of gold. Upon returning to the hotel, we adjourned to the bar for one more cocktail, where I also checked in on Facebook:

Despite it being a workday tomorrow, Mr Daley won't let me go to bed ... OK, then ... one more drink! —at Park Plaza Westminster Bridge

Heading to work the next morning, I received various texts from people enquiring how I met Tom Daley and how jammy I was. Sadly, though, I had to reply that the alcohol had been making me talk bollocks and I did not share a cocktail with a recent Olympic medal winner. Maybe I would one day, eh?

So the games finished with huge success, leaving me filled with pride that we as a nation pulled it off. But it left me wanting more. I reminisced back to what James had said at my birthday and thought why not complete an athletic challenge in each Olympic city before the next Olympics in Rio and document it on a blog? I would certainly be interested in reading a story like that if someone else did it, so surely others runners (and maybe some non-runners) would enjoy hearing about it too.

Regardless of whether others were interested, I thought, *Fuck it*. What a way to stay fit and travel (two of my favourite pastimes).

So on Monday, 20 August 2012 I set up the blog www. runalltheolympics.blogspot.co.uk and the challenge was set. I was going to create my own Olympic story, even if I wasn't good enough to compete in the actual games. The target was to compete in all previous twenty-two cities and finish in Rio in the year the city was to host the games (2016), so there would be twenty-three cities in all.

Here is my story of each city.

Chapter 2

Athens – The Birthplace of the Marathon (and Me)

Olympic years: 1896 and 2004
Athens Olympic fact: In the first Olympics, 241
athletes competed, all of which were men.

Once upon a time (as all fairy tales start), I was a beer monster at university, even winning an award for biggest party animal in my final year. How proud my parents must have been after years of expensive education! However, I eventually become a little more interested in getting fit and losing my beer belly. I couldn't get away with still calling it puppy fat in my late twenties.

Back in 2006, I entered the Great North Run and thoroughly enjoyed the training and the day itself. Afterwards, I wanted to keep my newly found fitness level going and completed other events like the London Triathlon, London to Paris bike ride, and London to Brighton bike ride, but lately I had been intrigued to see if I could do a marathon. Immediately, I thought of the one in Athens for three reasons:

1. The historical route running from Marathon to Athens is where modern-day marathons stem from.
2. It finished in the stunning Olympic stadium used in the first modern Olympic Games.
3. I was born in Athens and hadn't been back since I was eighteen.

In March 2010, I entered the run. There was no going back. I had eight months to be ready to run a marathon. I started training based on the suggested plan on the official Athens Marathon website, and my weekly regime consisted of four runs a week. Mondays, Wednesdays, and Fridays were always the same in length and finished off with a longer run on Sundays.

I quickly began to see progress and started to build up my midweek runs until, after a couple of months, they were seven miles each. I was enjoying the training, and my clothes were fitting me better – a nice bonus and an excuse to go shopping for new clothes.

October came and it was time to head out to Athens. I was looking forward to going back (especially with my mum and dad in tow), so I was not nervous at all. Arriving in the city was nostalgic and exciting. The captain on the plane welcomed us to Athens and wished those runners amongst us good luck in the race and hoped we got a PB (personal best), a lovely touch which made me smile. As this was my first marathon, I was certainly guaranteed a PB, and I was now super excited for the days that lay ahead.

The day before the marathon, I registered for the race and picked up my number at the expo. I was surprised to see how many stalls and people there were, and it only added fuel to my fire. I wanted the race start time to arrive. I spent the rest of the day (well, not literally all day, but you know what I mean) on the Hop-on, Hop-off bus tour (now a bit of a tradition that I have the day before a run), thus resting my feet. When night-time came, I loaded up on pasta for dinner and went to bed fairly early, as the alarm was set for 3.30 a.m.

I was up before dawn broke and jumped on the bus to Marathon for the start. I began to enjoy the day as soon as the bus set off, as other runners spoke to each other of previous runs, giving advice and in general creating a team feeling. We all warmed up in the stadium at Marathon, and soon it was time to start. Traditional Greek music saw us off at the start line, which warmed me and made me smile before it drowned out beneath my playlist of manly cheesy pop tunes.

I knew that the first half of the marathon was uphill, so I had already set my goal of simply finishing and nothing more. I took it easy and just enjoyed the route and stuck to my plan of refuelling at every drink and food station. I did have to pass on the one where they were handing out Coca-Cola. Surely that would not be good mid-run.

I knew that around thirty kilometres, there was a steep hill and this was the hardest part of the course. At the base of the hill, I took my first (and last) carb gel in order to make it up to the summit. Despite the gels being flavoured orange or strawberry and so on, I just can't seem to become friends with them and we remained enigmas to each other for some years after. The taste left me feeling worse than when I took it so it took some time to let another one to pass my lips.

A miniscule disadvantage with the Athens marathon starting in Marathon is that your personal supporters can only pick one place from which to watch you, and why would they choose anything apart from the triumphant end in the stadium? So this far in, I decided I would like some personal support from someone back home, so I chose to "phone a friend" and dialled my BFF, Laura. She encouraged me on and said she could hear the crowd around me, and before I knew it, I was at the top of the hill. I was on the homeward stretch.

As I neared the stadium, I took off my headphones to take in the atmosphere fully. Just as I entered the stadium, there were Mum and Dad to my right. I stopped in front of them to have my photo taken, giving a thumbs up and a smile. Moving on, I crossed the finish line completely pleased with my result of four hours and fourteen minutes.

Shortly after finishing, I sent texts simply saying "I did it" to numerous people back home. As I waited to get my bag back (in a very chaotic Greek way), a woman told me to give it fifteen minutes and I would start to plan where my next marathon would be. I was not so sure.

Bag finally in hand, off I went to the hotel to shower and then stock up on one of the best Greek deserts I have *ever* had! I'm not sure if it was the need for sugar or if the hotel just genuinely served good food. Either way, I couldn't have been happier.

I thought I would feel incredibly stiff the next day, but I was pleasantly surprised. I was still feeling excited from my achievement the day before and was even OK to go visit my former primary school and meet some of my old teachers. When I arranged the visit and they asked me to come the day after the race, I thought they were nuts, as I wouldn't be able to walk, but I guess my training paid off. I was capable of putting one foot in front of the other without pain.

It was a great holiday, and I came home feeling fulfilled to have completed my first marathon in my birth city. However, little did I know at that point that it would form a key part in my global Olympic challenge.

Target: 23
Completed: 1

Chapter 3

London – A Decathlon of Events

Olympic years: 1908, 1948, and 2012
London Olympic fact: It's the only city to
host the Olympics three times.

Of course, living in London made it easy for me to have already "ticked" this city off the list. In keeping with the Olympic theme, here is a decathlon of events I have completed in London Town.

Ena: The London Marathon. I will tell you about this one, but not until the end of the book. Let's keep it secret for now. No peeking ahead. I mean it!

Dio: In 2008, I took part in the London Moonwalk. Walking a marathon starting at midnight wearing a bra (and raising money for breast cancer) seemed not only fun but not too difficult since I considered myself fairly fit. Well, let me tell you that that is not the case! This event remains the most difficult one I have ever done. Up to mile seventeen, I was thoroughly enjoying the night, but thereafter my lower back began to hurt and nothing I tried would ease it up. When running, if I were to think there were only nine miles left, I would have been thinking that at least it's over in an hour, but when you are walking that distance, it's more like another three hours. The finish line took *forever* to come, and when it did, I literally crossed it, took my medal, and fell asleep for half an hour on the grass in Hyde Park. I vowed never to do another marathon, which, given chapter 1, we know did not turn out to be true. I have since returned to the Moonwalk in May 2012 to try the half marathon distance again, finding it harder than I thought I would. Despite being a lot fitter than the first time I took part, my lower back was still ridiculously painful from mile three. I must add that this second attempt may have been jeopardized by my behaviour the night before, having only got home from G-A-Y disco at 6 a.m. on the day of the event. I actually had a personal training session a mere three hours later, at 9 a.m., and was only awakened by my trainer calling me at 9.15 to say he was outside the house. Cue me running outside in my underwear, shouting across the road that I would be ready in two minutes. Talk about trailer trash and poor preparation for a half marathon that night! I take my hat (and bra) off to the thousands of women who do this event every year, as it is ultra-difficult – well done, ladies!

Tria: To raise money for the UK charity Child Line, the charity organised an event called Step Change. The challenge was to climb the iconic Gherkin building in central London to the promise of champagne at the bar at the top after having scaled the 1,037 steps. I made it up to the top in six minutes and twenty-eight seconds (almost beating my parents, who took the lift). Champagne in hand, I enjoyed the views, canapés, and songs performed by the London Gay Men's Chorus.

Tessera: One of my favourite London events is the Great Drag Race for Prostate Action, a 10.2-kilometre run (representing the 10,200 men who lose their fight against prostate cancer in the UK each year) whereby all participants must run in drag. I always swore that I could never do a run in fancy dress, but for this cause, which is very close to my heart, I would make an exception. The first time I ran (2011), I transformed into the black swan, taking inspiration from the recent (and one of my favourite) film for my outfit. Throughout the race, I had been running close to a lovely-looking drag queen pretty much all the way round the course. Spectators apparently had been saying that the race was between us and had been wondering whether we would race it to the end and fight to the finish or simply cross the line together. We did race to the end, and the drag queen just beat me over the line, but I was happy thinking I had finished second. But no. It appeared that another queen had beaten us to it. Bitch! The race consists of ten circuits (which you need to count yourself) around Highbury Fields, and to this day, I am convinced he missed a lap, but still, a respectable third place was good enough for me.

Continuing with the bird theme the second year (2012), I went for a full-on flamingo ensemble. It was beautifully pink, skimpy, and something Cher would have killed for, I am sure. Determined to better my ranking, I did move up one notch to finish in second place – but still not beating the same winner from the year before. Perhaps he did count correctly in 2011, then. For my flamingo efforts, I did also gain an additional award for the best-looking geezer in drag, so again, I can't complain, and it was a nice way to celebrate what would have been my Dad's sixty-eighth birthday. He had lost his fight with prostate cancer just eleven days before the event. Sadly, the run no longer takes place, but who knows what position (and feathered outfit) a third attempt would have brought!

Pente: Supporting my local area, I entered the inaugural Ealing Half Marathon in 2012. It made such a refreshing change to be able to walk four minutes to the start line from my house, not having to rely on bag drops and knowing that once I finished, I would be minutes away from a hot shower. It was thoroughly enjoyable to run around the area I live in, and I finished in one hour, twenty-three minutes, and fourteen seconds, which was a personal best at the time, placing me forty-first out of around 4,600. I returned for the second Ealing Half Marathon in 2013, improving my time to one hour, twenty-one minutes, and thirty seconds, which I was pleased with despite having forgotten what a hilly area I live in! I decided that I would run this race every year from then on. Here are the subsequent results: 2014: one hour, twenty-three minutes, and thirty-three seconds (sixty-eighth out of 4,245). 2015: one hour, twenty-three minutes, and fifty-one seconds.

Exi: I finished 2012 with the six-kilometre Santa Dash in Battersea Park. Five thousand people running in Santa costumes was a brilliant sight (especially seeing everyone on the train heading to the start) and a great way to raise money for Disability Snowsport. My friends Claire and Laura agreed to take part in the run but warned me that they would not be running the entire route. My trainer had put on my running plan to "race it", which I was unsure of, as it didn't seem like the kind of event in which to be competitive. Moreover, racing with a beard and huge jacket was not ideal. I parted company with the girls not long after the first five hundred metres and dashed to the finish in twenty-six minutes. Upon waiting for the girls at the end, they were most disappointed to learn that a man with a broken leg had beaten them! A good start to a festive day, though. Footnote (literally): Claire asked me to mention that the man with the broken limb was using a scooter for his unwell leg to rest on, so therefore he had an advantage over her and Laura. End of footnote.

Epta: In 2013, group buying website Living Social organised a run to raise money for the Comic Relief charity. The course was set as a five-kilometre route through central London, crossing the impressive Tower Bridge. As an added bit of fun, it was called the Onesie Dash, meaning all competitors would have to wear a onesie. It was a great event for a great cause and turned out to be the run with all the ones for the following reasons. It was the one and only time I have ever worn a onesie, plus I managed to finish in first place, making me King of the Onesies for the day.

Octo: After the Athens Marathon, alongside continuing my running, I had decided to start seeing a personal trainer in order to build my core strength. I really felt the benefits of this in my running results but also enjoyed my sessions. During one session, my trainer and I were talking about crazy events around the world and the topic of the Tough Mudder came up. Tough Mudder is an 11.5-mile run through mud and uneven terrain, with twenty-one obstacles along the way. It is marketed as "probably the toughest event on the planet". My trainer suggested that we consider entering together, as we would make a good team, for he clearly was physically strong and I had stamina to keep us going along the running part of the event. I thought, *Why not?* So we signed up.

Only after doing this did I research the actual obstacles. They included fire, ice baths, fifteen-foot walls, and electricity. Shit the bed. What had I gotten myself into! Training-wise we were fit enough to do it (him especially), but I was troubled by a couple of things, namely crawling and running through water whilst getting electric shocks and signing a form actually called a "death waiver" prior to being allowed to collect my race number. The night before the event, I was extremely nervous, not feeling like that since the eve of my first half marathon (the Great North Run) back in 2006. It was an early start to drive to the location, which was billed as "South London" but was actually Winchester; however, given the difficulty of the event, I still like to include it here as a London event.

As the morning went on, I started to relax a little. Upon arrival at the site, the atmosphere was electric, literally a sign of things to come. I chilled out a little during the warm-up but then was somewhat worried when I struggled to get over the warm-up wall before the start. How the fuck was I going to make it over the real obstacles? What kept me going was the real sense of camaraderie at the start line and that everyone was really in the event to help each other get through it. If need be, someone (i.e., my trainer) would need to push me over each obstacle.

Once we were under way, I relaxed and found that the first obstacles were not as bad as I had been expecting. I was enjoying climbing walls, crawling through mud under barbed wire, jumping into pools of water from a great height, and crawling under tanks and in tunnels. One I hadn't been so worried about was the "funky monkey" – I mean monkey bars. How hard could that be? I used to love them as a child. However, the problem was that I hadn't actually done them since childhood. I got about halfway across when I made the grave error of holding on to the bar with both hands. I knew there was no way out and hung there for a few seconds like Reverend Scott at the end of *The Poseidon Adventure* and then let go, falling into another pool of murky water.

The only obstacle I found amazingly tough physically was where we needed to carry a log between us for what felt like a mile but was in fact probably about five hundred metres. Before I knew it, we arrived at the "electric eel" obstacle.

It was a shallow pool about twenty metres long, with electric cables hanging above it. Essentially, you had to move on your belly through the pool, trying to avoid the cables. I quickly found out that I was not good at this, and second by second, I seemed to be getting shocked, making my language progressively worse as I moved each inch. Apparently quite amusing to hear, according to my trainer ahead of me, who was remaining amazingly shock-free. Making it through, I was relieved and continued to enjoy the other things in our path.

Not much later, we made it to the final one, situated at the finish line: "Electroshock therapy". More electricity? I had to stop to gather my thoughts before running through the barrage of cables that stood between me and the end. Egged on by the crowd, I made a run for it and again experienced shocks that I would not want to repeat, but it was worth it. I received my Tough Mudder headband and a pint of Strongbow. Despite being so nervous before the event, I thoroughly enjoyed it and am pleased as punch to have done it. Perhaps a career in the army is not out of the question should things in the travel industry go wrong. Michael equals one tough fairy and I have the coveted orange headband to prove it.

Ennea: In contrast to the Tough Mudder, the Color Run promises to be the "happiest five kilometres on the planet", so how could I resist taking place in the inaugural one in London? The Color Run craze started in the United States, hence the spelling of *color* (without a *u* in it), and has proven so popular that the event is popping up everywhere globally. The run is purely focused on fun and adopts only two rules:

1. Wear white at the starting line
2. Finish plastered in colour

It was refreshing to take part in an event where a timing chip is not even given out, and the energy at the start line was fantastic. The run in London took us around the outside of Wembley Stadium, and at each kilometre marker, volunteers would shower us with different coloured paint. We were told that the paint was sugar based, which sounded even better to me. Should I get hungry and need an energy boost along the way, I could simply lick myself. Yum. The day in London was absolutely scorching, but it was a fantastic event and I did manage to run it sub-twenty minutes, stopping to ensure I obeyed rule number two and finished covered in a multitude of colours. I would certainly encourage families the world over to enter and enjoy it together.

Deka: Did you know that a group of tigers is called a streak of tigers? So in order to raise money and awareness to protect the endangered Sumatran tiger (of which there are only three hundred left in the wild), London Zoo put on an event called Streak for Tigers. It required me to drop everything (literally) and streak through the zoo. Yes, I would be required to run completely naked. For a few seconds, I thought about how daunting that may be, but then I thought, *Sod it.* Why not enter and prove that I am not only Long by name but long by nature! I signed up and only had a few days to go before the "big" event.

Turning up there was a good buzz, and the volunteers had highlighted the way to the start line/"changing area" with underwear in the trees, which was definitely unique. As I entered the runners' area, I was quite surprised to see that there were quite a large percentage of the 250 strong group already standing around naked. It seemed there were only a few using their running foils to cover up until the start so clearly some had much more experience at this naturist thing than I did. I registered and was shown to the male changing room. Why was there a need for separate rooms for men and women since we had to come out of the rooms naked and see each other anyway?

This fact was clear at the end, when it seemed that many people were changing in the wrong room!

I undressed and went out to the start area (my waist down covered by the foil), which was out of sight of the spectators. What I wasn't expecting was to be given tiger cupcakes and four shots (one each of rum, vodka, gin, and tequila) from the bar. Clearly, they knew what a lot of us needed in order to get going! I made friends with another runner who was by himself. He wasn't too nervous and seemed to be more embarrassed to say where he worked than why he decided to enter the event. His place of work was RBS. It all made sense when he told me, given the recent bad publicity of the banking industry.

Soon after the downing of many shots, we were lined up behind a set of curtains and the countdown began. The curtains were thrown open and the spectators got a full view of us all as we ran off into the zoo. The run was fun, and albeit short (three hundred metres), it felt liberating and perhaps the way to run from then on. (Don't worry – the rest of the book does not continue the naked theme.) I finished the streak quite tipsy and celebrated with a Tiger beer, pleased to have also raised just over two hundred pounds for the cause.

Target: 23
Completed: 2

Chapter 4

Tokyo – Please Let Me Run with You

Olympic year: 1964
Tokyo Olympic fact: The Olympic flame was lit by
Yoshinori Sakai, who was born in Hiroshima the day
the atomic bomb was dropped on the city.

BFF Laura and I had organised a week's holiday in Tokyo during August 2012, and our plans included karaoke, sushi, Disneyland, Hello Kitty Town, and perhaps a little training in the hotel gym (which incidentally afforded splendid views over the city from its rooftop location).

However, I had set my Olympic challenge only three weeks before heading to Japan. I then realized that Tokyo was one of my target cities and it was unlikely I would be there again prior to 2016.

What to do?

As usual, I reached out to everyone's firm friend: Google. Results of half marathons, ten kilometres, and marathons in Tokyo were plentiful, but there were none in the seven days I would be there. I then stumbled across a local running club website (http://www.

namban.org/index.php/about/club) and dropped them a note to see if they knew of any upcoming events that week.

To my surprise and delight, they replied almost instantaneously, saying that due to it being summer, there weren't any competitive races. However, they were having a five-kilometre time trial at their track on one of the days I was there, and if I wanted to come along, I could; that would be my Tokyo run.

How great was that?

So on the plane out to Tokyo (luckily being in upper class on Virgin Atlantic) I sat at the bar and couldn't contain my excitement of properly starting my challenge and letting those at the bar know that not only would I be soaking up the Japanese culture but also running. One shit-faced woman was so impressed that she offered to sponsor me ahead of my challenge and asked me to give her my details before we disembarked in Tokyo. Shortly after this conversation, she adjourned to her flat bed and passed out for the rest of the flight. She simply looked at me at immigration as though she vaguely recognized me but couldn't quite work out why. No details were exchanged, and no sponsorship came my way. Crazy drunk. That's me – not her – by the way. I guess that's what happens when you spend eight hours out of a twelve-hour flight at the bar.

Tokyo was everything and more than I expected. Busy. Colourful. Friendly, Exciting. Different. We did all the expected activities. Shopping in Harajuku. Seeing the Ginza district. Getting the odd unexpected douching on a Japanese high-tech toilet. We visited Tokyo Disneyland and Sanrio Puroland (or Hello Kitty Town, as I prefer to call it). Having been to five (out of six, now that Shanghai has just opened) Disney parks (Los Angeles, Orlando, Paris, Hong Kong, and Tokyo), I can safely say that the Japanese family member is by far the craziest. Everyone (and I literally mean every other visitor) was dressed head to toe in Disney gear. This includes all the adults. I have never seen so many people embrace the Disney brand so much. I am sure the park could stay open and profitable based purely on their merchandising sales alone. Hello Kitty Town, on the other hand, was much more geared towards the children. It was a hilarious day and a must-see when in Japan.

My advice for the day goes like this. Go out drinking in a karaoke bar the night before and arrive back at your hotel at 4am pleased with your performance of power balads and minus your belly button ring. It was probably about time I stopped wearing that anyway since I was no longer a teen (or in my twenties.) We arrived in the park later that day, which is underground and without any daylight. There were lights. There were characters. There was Japanese music. Laura asked me if it was the parade. I had no idea there was a parade. She reminded me that I had said in the wee hours of the night before that I wasn't prepared to miss the parade and we should be up early. I guess we didn't miss it, then. Seeing Laura's hungover face of excitement as we entered Kitty's bedroom was a gem. Her delight was entirely because she got to have a lie-down on the bed and not down to simply being in Kitty's residence. We surely weren't the average visitors but do go and visit it.

The night before I had planned to meet the running club, Laura and I decided to stay in one of the capsule hotels which are famous throughout Japan. What could go wrong with sleeping in your own individual pod? Surely a great way to immerse ourselves into the Japanese culture. We checked in and were shown the traditional onsen bathroom. It was awesome. Relaxed, I went to view my capsule. It was cute. It had its own TV. I loved it. I said goodnight to Laura and we would meet at breakfast.

It was midnight when we went to bed, and lying in my capsule, I began to think a little about the run and how exciting it would be to complete city number three. However, after about half an hour, I began to realize that being quite tall and not fitting completely in the bed was a slight comfort issue. Even more troublesome was the heat. As the mercury seemed to continue to rise, I lay there all night thinking that surely I would pass out soon and at least rest that way, but no. I think I managed approximately one hour in what felt like a mini-oven before the alarm went off. I was cooked.

I wasn't particularly worried, as I knew I could survive on little sleep so we carried on with a day of sightseeing. It wasn't until about an hour before we were meeting the running club that my eyes began to fade and I suggested we stop for a juice, to which Laura agreed. We sat at a street side cafe, where I promptly downed my drink and fell asleep at the table. To passers-by, it may have looked like a first date that perhaps was not going too well.

My next error of the day was that I had arranged to meet the club manager at a central metro station. In order to make meeting easy, I had said I would be wearing my Team GB tracksuit (fresh from London 2012). I thought that was one way to easily be spotted. As I mentioned, it was not chilly while we were in Japan, but I had to wear it in order for him to find me. So there I was in a crowded metro station looking very British in my tracksuit and sweating profusely. Upon meeting, the tracksuit came straight off. Fear not, I did have clothes on underneath it.

At the track, I met the thirty or so other regular runners. They consisted of expatriates from all corners of the globe as well as some locals. They were all keen runners, with some having achieved some impressive marathon times in the Tokyo race earlier that year. They were approachable and welcoming. I was officially introduced to them during our warm-up stretches. There was a young boy (if I had to guess, I'd say he was about twelve years old) who was also new to the club that week. He was English but lived in Tokyo. His mum had brought him along to try out the club. I could tell he was a little nervous being surrounded by adults who knew each other, so I offered to do our warm-up laps together, which he was grateful for. Talking to him and his mum before the time trial, I discovered they were moving back to the UK at the end of the year and had just bought a house in the street opposite my mum. Disney was right: It's a small world after all. But I digress.

The five-kilometre race itself was good fun and was actually the first time I had run properly on a track. Twelve and a half times round the track is quite a lot of circles to complete. I did it, though, with a time of nineteen minutes and two seconds, which was a five-kilometre best for me at the time and a good result given the humidity. Whilst it felt good to be running on a track and with quite a few people watching, I still prefer races to be out on the street and seeing the city along the way. For me, doing circuits is much more tiring mentally. I like runs that finish at a stadium for a final lap, but I do find it difficult running an entire race on a track.

Everyone at the Tokyo running club was so kind. After the time trial, we went to a curry house for dinner. It was a fun night, and I am forever grateful that they helped me achieve the Tokyo part of my challenge.

I thanked them and Laura, and I went off to check into a love hotel for the night. That's not as naughty as it sounds, though. No, really, it's not.

Target: 23

Completed: 3

Chapter 5

Stockholm – Come Join the Joyride

Olympic year: 1912
Stockholm Olympic fact: These were the first games
to include aquatic events for women.

At the end of 2011, I took on a new role at work. I was managing the affiliate programme for the European markets of the company website. In turn, this would require me to travel to various places throughout the year for partner meetings. Scandinavia was a key market for the company, so I was due to take a trip to visit some of the teams there soon. Whilst planning a trip to Stockholm with my client, he mentioned that the Stockholm half marathon was on in September. Why not come over then? I could run the race and follow it up with a couple of days' work. Perfect.

I had the trip to Stockholm planned (in my head and not actually booked at this point) when I met up with the rest of the Scandinavian teams in Oslo. During a rather drunken night out in Oslo (which involved drinks at a client's office at 4 a.m. whilst playing with a large stuffed Angry Bird), I mentioned the upcoming Stockholm trip to my Finnish client. She told me she had run a half marathon in Helsinki around the same time last year and if I gave her a second she would check with our global friend Google to see when this year's race was. There it was – the following weekend to the Stockholm one. Why not go out to Stockholm to run the race, work in Stockholm for two days, and then travel to Helsinki to work for the rest of the week and finish up (no pun intended) with a half marathon in Helsinki? It was all too good a plan to pass up. It was all placed firmly in the diary.

A few months later, I arrived in Stockholm. Incidentally, it is one of my favourite cities. I was ready to see some of the sights again and eat some meatballs. If you can't get to Sweden, then just try the Ikea ones. Trust me – they are good. It was fairly chilly, but the sky was a brilliant bright blue, a wonderful way to see this city, particularly as it is made up of hundreds of islands so the sunlight bouncing off the water is a beautiful sight to see. In addition, the brisk air gave me a nice excuse to have many hot chai lattes (accompanied by cake) in order to stay warm and race ready. All athletes do that before important meets. No? Well, maybe they should.

At race registration, I picked up my number. I purchased a new running top sporting the Swedish flag colours. I was dressed for success (Roxette pun totally intended) and ready for my next half marathon. The event was well organized, and there were about seventeen thousand runners gathered at the start line just in front of the Royal Palace on Gamla Stan island.

The race got off to a great start. I was pleased with the progress I was making, and it felt like this could be my best time ever. I was a little warm in my new long-sleeved top but unzipping it allowed some cold refreshing Nordic air to hit my neck. It felt good. At around seventeen kilometres, suddenly I began to think ahead about how far I had to go. At my current pace, what time would I finish in? This was the first half marathon I had run with the markers being in kilometres rather than miles. In my head, I had that the race was twenty-four kilometres total rather than the 21,098 kilometres that it actually is. As I began to work out my time per kilometre, I started to think I was actually running slower than I had thought and I would actually be about on track for the same time I had done in my previous best race (Edinburgh in one hour and twenty-seven minutes). I was still going to be pleased with my result and simply let my beloved Roxette's back catalogue help me along the way. Being an unashamed uberfan, I even recognised places where some of their videos where filmed. I was enjoying every moment when, to my surprise, I saw Steven in the crowd. He told me he was going to be waiting just before the finish line. Then came the eight hundred meters to go marker. Could it be that I was mistaken and was about to beat my own PB? Yes. I crossed the line in one hour, twenty-six minutes, and eighteen seconds, placing me 289th. I was thrilled.

That afternoon, I celebrated by going to the spirit (as in alcohol, not scary ghosts) museum, followed by a few expensive vodkas in a bar, where, to my further delight, they played a Roxette song. A little tipsy I wandered back to my hotel via the heated statue that stands outside the opera house for a warm cuddle. I tell everyone about this statue, and even many locals don't believe it exists. I promise you it does. I haven't just imagined hugging something warm and bronze on the street.

The entire day and weekend only deepened my love of Swedish culture, and it was one more city done. Despite being a "new" runner, I think Roxette summed it up nicely in one of my favourite songs of theirs when they said, "Seems like I've been running, all my life, like watercolours in the rain."

So on to a couple of days of work and then to the airport to head straight to Helsinki for the next race, leaving only one last thing to do before I boarded the plane: buying a chocolate bar called Plopp, a local delicacy. It reduces me to a childish snigger every time I see one or think of it.

Target: 23
Completed: 4

Chapter 6

Helsinki – The Beach Run

Olympic year: 1952
Helsinki Olympic fact: These were the first
games in which the USSR competed.

On to Helsinki it was. It was a city I had been to before, but I am a sucker for Scandinavian design, so it was a pleasant place to be back.

This time the weather was more of what you may expect in September in Scandinavia. Lots. Of. Rain.

I checked into my central hotel and thought I would go for a training run before dinner. There was no gym in the hotel. A little rain never hurt anyone, and I knew the city well enough not to get lost. So off I went and made my way down to the waterfront, where I followed the path along the coast. I passed statues, traditional Finnish huts, as well as the occasional runner. I am polite (excluding my language), so I nodded and smiled as I went past each fellow jogger. In return, I only received slightly worried looks back from them. Perhaps acknowledging others is not the thing to do in Finland.

I carried on and arrived back at the hotel feeling ready for a shower prior to a spot of nourishment. I walked past reception, where the same guy who had checked me in was manning the desk. He was currently checking in a new group of guests. He stopped speaking with them and asked me if I was OK, if I had gotten lost. Of course not. I had thoroughly enjoyed my run, thank you very much. Once again, I received a slightly puzzled look, this time from the receptionist.

It wasn't until I reached my room that I then looked in the full-length mirror and realized why this was happening to me. The red dye from the new headphones I had bought had rubbed off onto my white top in the rain. Not only that but it had also strategically decided to run down my top from the exact place where my nipples were. The dye went all the way down my six-pack. OK, tummy. The concerned looks from the locals now made sense. I appeared to be a smiling man running whilst his nipples were bleeding. Overall, it probably was not the best way to make a positive impression with the community. Well, that outside of the S&M community anyway. More on that later. I'm just kidding.

Nipples still intact, I spent the next day checking out the Olympic stadium. It was built in 1940 in the popular art deco style of the time in preparation for the games, but due to World War II, the games never took place. The stadium was used eventually when Finland played host to the games in 1952. The stadium has an impressive viewing tower which affords fantastic views of inside the stadium as well as the surrounding city (especially since the day I was up there was rain-free). It was a perfect way to get revved up for a race the next day.

The run was actually called the Rantamaraton, which translates as the beach marathon and is held in the Helsinki neighbourhood of Espoo.

I was up early to get the bus to the start line (in the returned rain) but this time wearing a black top just in case my headphones should pull the same trick from two days prior. On arrival, the two thousand runners were in good spirits despite the weather. It was again organized with super Scandinavian efficiency. I am still always a little embarrassed that the registration team were able to help me with everything in English. I can't help but think of whether this service is returned when International runners come to events in the UK. With regret, I don't think it is.

After a chilly and wet wait for the gun, I was running quickly and appeared to be keeping up with the leaders of the race. The route was along some roads but also through woods, with the water and coastline always in sight. It was an attractive route but undoubtedly would have been more pleasant in the sunshine. I focused on getting to the end simply to get warm; however, once again, I realized that perhaps I could be on track to better my result from seven days earlier in Stockholm. When realizing you are in reach of achieving a personal best, it takes even more concentration to stay focused and maintain the pace you have been going. The importance of concentration was never more apparent than at that exact moment when I took a wrong turn. Oops. After only about twenty seconds or so of running on my own did I realize I had to turn back. Annoyed with myself, I then lost hope of a PB and just went back to dreaming of wearing warm dry clothes.

I reached the racetrack where we had started and continued as hard as I could to the end, where again I could see Steven.

Result: one hour, twenty-five minutes, and fifty seconds, placing me twentieth

I was surprised with my time. The devil in me couldn't help but think if only I hadn't gone wrong, I would have been even quicker. Nonetheless, I was chuffed and I could go home to London pleased that within the space of a week, I had beaten my PB. Twice. And I had ticked off a further two Olympic cities for my challenge. Celebrations that night were in the form of pizza and pints of a gin-based drink. The locals made me drink it. I didn't mind, to be honest. Marvellous.

Target: 23
Completed: 5

Chapter 7

Istanbul – One Foot in Asia and One in Europe

Prior to coming up with this challenge, I had already entered a fifteen-kilometre run in Istanbul. Whilst running in such a fascinating city, it also appealed to me that the race started in Asia and finished in Europe. Pretty cool to be able to say that in one day I ran between two continents.

It then transpired that Istanbul was actually a candidate city for the 2020 Olympics, so it felt right that I could still include it here as an Olympic run even though technically it isn't an Olympic city. The race started early, so I was up at dawn with the aid of a natural alarm in the form of the morning prayer call from the mosque just behind my hotel room. Race day included a five-kilometre run, a fifteen-kilometre run, and a marathon, all part of the same event. Before you think of me as some ultra-hero, I wasn't running all of them. I was opting for the fifteen-kilometre one.

To reach the start line, a short bus ride was required from the old town centre. Upon arrival at the start area, I could see the start marker for the marathon and the five kilometre farther up the hill, but no fifteen kilometre. I hoped that I hadn't gotten on the wrong bus and quickly asked a fellow runner, who confirmed that yes, it would be starting from this area too. But where? My runner companion was from Istanbul and said that the race was probably running by Turkish timelines and they would put the marker up at the last minute. Sure enough, about fifteen minutes before kick-off, the fifteen-kilometre arch started to be inflated. Talking to her a little more, I asked if she was excited about her city potentially hosting the games. She said there was a fair amount of support for the bid but that many people felt that they would not be ready in time should the bid be successful. I guessed that today was no exception.

With seconds to spare, the race was off. Down the hill we sped and across the long bridge over the river to Europe. The run itself was much hillier than I anticipated, but I took in some fantastic views of the mighty Bosphorus. Running up into the old town and finishing by the Blue Mosque was one of the most scenic ends to a race I have had the pleasure of experiencing. I thought it was well organised despite the hiccup at the start, and I was thinking that Istanbul would make a great Olympic city.

At the end of the race, I came home in fifty-first place out of about four thousand, in a time of one hour and fifteen seconds, gutted not to be under the one-hour mark. Maybe next time.

I was in Amsterdam for my Olympic challenge (September 2013) when it was announced that Tokyo had won its bid to host the 2020 Olympics, meaning that Istanbul was not to be. For selfish reasons, part of me had wanted Madrid (the third candidate city in the running) to be successful, as it would mean another city for me to run in. However, I have no doubt that Tokyo will put on a spectacular show, and I guess it means that I will still have competed in every Summer Olympics city right up until the summer of 2020.

Chapter 8

Barcelona – The Run with All the *B*s ... Bad Back, Blisters, and Bruises

---

Olympic year: 1992
Barcelona Olympic fact: It was the first time in twenty years that there was no official boycott by a nation.

December and Christmas 2012 had been a bit wild for me. I said to myself that I am rather healthy most months of the year, so why not end the year with a complete blowout? Numerous parties, mince pies, countless shots, inappropriate Facebook check-ins and tags later, and it was approaching February and time for my next Olympic half marathon. I had been continuing to train throughout the festive period but didn't quite feel in top shape. I knew I could still make it round the course, but it possibly wasn't going to be the most impressive time.

However, two weeks before the run, disaster struck, and left me thinking I would not be running at all. Leaving a meeting at work and laden down with my notepad, pen, and drink, I stopped by the little boys' room on the way back to my desk. As I walked in, I dropped my cup, and in my haste not to let it hit the floor, I bent over quickly to stop it. As I did, not only did I miss the cup, allowing its contents to go everywhere, but my back seized and I felt a sharp pain the entire way down the lower right hand side. Great. I was in the work toilets and bent over behind someone at the urinal, trying not to yelp in pain. I was unable to stand, plus my spilt drink was covering the floor behind him. Nice way to say good morning to the vice president of HR, who happened to be the one standing at the urinal.

Composing my thoughts, I played up to the British stereotype and said I was fine, whilst actually inside I was crying. A lot. After a painful afternoon and evening, I went for acupuncture the following day during my lunch hour, which helped and loosened the muscles, but when dusk came, I could feel it getting worse again. The only way I could think of to beat it at this point was to drink copious amounts of cava and then hit the dance floor of a local club. This must be a sure-fire way to ensure my back loosens up, right? Of course it wasn't. By the following Monday, I was barely able to walk or even sit down, so I was beginning to think that this would spell the end of my impending Barcelona run. In my desperation, I went to see another physiotherapist during my lunch hour at work. Within one fairly expensive session, he had me walking normally. He gave me exercises to relax my back and assured me I would be OK to try running (albeit gently) in a few days. Sticking to his advice a few days later, I went for a gentle jog, and to my delight, my back was fine and I no longer felt the pain from the previous few days. Money totally well spent.

With my back under control, I was then back on track (pun intended) for Barcelona and bought some new trainers ahead of the race. My first training run in the new gear went well, but in the last few minutes, I could feel a slight rubbing on one of my heels, which is nothing I have not experienced before. However, upon getting home and removing said trainers, to my horror, rather than blisters, I found no skin on either of my heels. Straight away I knew it would be agony putting any kind of shoes back on over my heels, and I wondered how could this happen without my noticing. Within seconds, I was then back once again thinking that Barcelona was going to be a no-go. I forced some shoes on and hobbled to work. Lunchtimes in the run up to Barcelona were proving to be very useful, and this time it saw me heading to the running shop (getting the bus, as I couldn't walk the five hundred metres) and begging for help. They gave me anti-blister stickers to put in my trainers and recommended some specific plasters (my introduction to what will be a lifelong relationship with Compeed) along with wearing anti-blister socks. I bought everything they threw at me. It was a great day for them if they were working on commission. Once I put the plasters on, I realized they effectively become your new layer of skin; I felt a little better already.

To let my feet heal, I didn't run for the rest of the week and wore my trainers all the time to wear them in. Ordinarily I am firmly a dedicated follower of fashion so going out in public in running trainers (whilst not running) was a big step for me and clearly a sign of desperation that I wanted my feet to be well for the weekend.

I got to Barcelona. I had some nice tapas and then realised I had forgotten to bring my tracksuit and training bag with me. Reading this, you would almost think I was a complete running novice. I quickly bought some outer clothes – otherwise, the race morning would have been rather chilly – and then partook in a day of sightseeing (on an open-top bus), having decided just to enjoy the race the next day. I hadn't run for two weeks and had put a PB out of my mind. After Helsinki, I had taken part in the inaugural Ealing half marathon and had come in forty-first place out of four thousand, in a time of one hour, twenty-three minutes, and fourteen seconds, so this was the new time to beat.

With my feet and back feeling fine and dandy, I lined up at the start of the race with the one-hour, twenty-minute pacemaker, with the intention of staying with him for around ten to twelve kilometres and then dropping back to my own pace, where I could at least try to equal my latest time from London.

All was going swimmingly and the pace didn't seem too much of a stretch for me, so I truly began to enjoy the race. At five kilometres, the first water stop was coming up, so I broke away slightly from the pacemaker group moving to the right and got a bottle of water. I hadn't even taken a sip when suddenly from behind me I felt someone catch my heel and send me hurtling forwards onto the road. In shock, I jumped up and carried on running (minus the water bottle), somehow not losing any ground from the pacemaker. My hands were stinging but on inspection didn't seem cut, but I could see that my knees were bleeding. This time it definitely was not just the dye from my headphones. I continued to run, thinking that if I didn't stop, it wouldn't hurt. For the third time in just as many weeks, I wondered if this could finally be the end of my Barcelona race.

Various concerned runners asked if I was OK, and the guy who accidently tripped me was apologetic and shared his water with me, for which I was grateful. As I carried on, I realized that whilst I may have cut knees, the pain was OK, and I kept up with the group until around thirteen kilometres and then let them go ahead as planned.

I continued with the race and then realized that soon I was only one kilometre from the end and well within my one-hour, twenty-three minute target. I pushed on through as hard as I could and then crossed the finish line in one hour, twenty minutes, and seven seconds, placing me in 225th out of 14,325. A new PB!

I couldn't believe after the run up to the race and even factoring a fall that I had managed to achieve this time. The pacemaker must have been going slightly faster than the intended finish time. Crossing the line with my pink-tinged socks, I was ecstatic. Waiting for me in the finishers' area, I saw the man who'd tripped me. It was a terrific show of sportsmanship for him to wait to apologise again and to congratulate me on my result.

A happy me celebrated with paella by the harbour, sporting even more plaster but this time on my knees instead of my feet.

Target: 23
Completed: 6

Chapter 9

Rome – The Run That Went Missing

Olympic year: 1960
Rome Olympic fact: It was the only Olympics in which
Cassius Clay (later known as Muhammad Ali) took part.

Following Barcelona the next weekend, I was all booked to head to Rome for the half marathon. Could this be another PB?

Being in the perfect place to stock up on carbs via pizza and pasta, what could have been better the following day than running the half marathon going past the Coliseum, amongst other world-famous sights, and finishing on an Italian beach in Ostia?

About two weeks prior to the race, I thought I would check the course, so I went to the website to discover this message in the header: "Save the new date – 3/3/13".

What the actual fuck?

Surely the date couldn't just randomly change without telling the runners? As per the T-shirt that Madonna once sported – "Italians do it better" – I presumed this would extend to the organization of an International run which would attract runners from all corners of the globe. But after a frantic email questioning that I must be mistaken about what I read, I received the following response:

> *Hi … Unfortunately, the Italian government decided to run the election day 24 February and we had to move the race to the next Sunday, 3 March. Hope this is not a problem for you.*

Not a problem? Were they kidding? Of course it was a problem. I had booked non-refundable flights, plus my hotel. In addition, hadn't they known about the election date for months? After a little rant (to myself) and determined not to be beaten, I reached out to Google once more, and within an hour, I had organized a private run with a company that did running tours around Rome (www.sightjogging. it). A run in the Olympic city of Rome was back on.

I arrived in Rome and was still excited for what lay ahead. I was staying in an apartment near the Vatican and quickly discovered a little cafe nearby, where the owner was kind enough to make me a hearty breakfast each morning consisting of scrambled eggs, toast, and a bowl of muesli, despite it not even being on the menu.

Sunday came round, and it was time for my tour. My running guide, David, was American and had lived in the city for four years, having studied there and leading tours of the Vatican as well. He met me at my hotel at nine on the Sunday morning and took me on a ten-kilometre run around the city, taking in sights like the Coliseum, Tomb of the Unknown Soldier, Castle di Angelo, Piazza Novono, and over some beautiful bridges with stunning views of the Tiber and St. Peter's Basilica. This was following a day of sightseeing (on an open-top bus) in torrential rain, so it was more than pleasant to be experiencing what felt like an almost empty city under bright blue sunshine. David stopped a couple of times to drink from the water fountains around the city, and I asked if I was going too fast for him, to which he replied I wasn't. Liar. He did say, though, that it was nice that he was leading someone who wasn't almost walking. A small dig at previous clients or just making himself feel better? I did ease up the pace a little after that.

I thoroughly enjoyed the run, and I would recommend it to anyone as a way to take in the city and the sights. Doing it on a Sunday morning meant that the city was still only waking up and allowed me to run with little traffic and get some excellent photos of the attractions that are ordinarily swamped with tourists.

Getting back to my hotel, I felt energized for the rest of the day and would definitely be looking up jogging tours in other cities I visited in the future. To follow a successful morning, it also turned out that Pope Benedict XVI would be giving his last Sunday blessing from the Vatican at midday. So after a spot of breakfast at my weekend local, I headed down to St. Peter's Square to watch him speak in numerous languages to the many pilgrims who had come to see him. It felt special to be there on that day, knowing that in over six hundred years, no pope had resigned and done what he was doing at that moment. There were many emotional religious figures in the crowd, and despite my not being religious, it still felt rather moving to be there.

For the rest of the day, I met up with an old school friend (thanks to the power of Facebook) I hadn't seen for over ten years, who was now living and working in Rome. We drank wine, ate pasta, and caught up on many years of gossip. She also drove me around town on her Vespa, making me feel uber-local. A particular highlight of our "road trip" was when she parked the scooter and, as we continued to jabber, managed to lock up someone else's bike rather than her own. Needless to say, said bike's owner was not as amused as we were upon our return to the bikes three hours later. Oops. Oh well, what can you do other than apologise, laugh, and drive off into the sunset?

So Rome didn't quite turn out to be the half marathon I had planned, but nonetheless, it was still a fantastic run and turned out to be a weekend where I felt quite like a local for forty-eight hours. Perhaps it was also best to have a break from such a long race, as the half marathon in Paris was coming up in a mere seven days' time.

Target: 23
Completed: 7

Chapter 10

Paris – "Du Pain, Pas de Vin, du Boursin"

Olympic years: 1900 and 1924
Paris Olympic fact: The film Chariots of Fire *is*
centred around the 1924 Paris Games.

Paris is also one of my favourite cities. I know it fairly well, so I was excited to have it on the Olympic hit list. I was nervous upon entering the half marathon, as I knew it involved having to provide a medical certificate from your doctor stating you were fit to run. It may sound crazy, but I was worried that this would be an issue for me to get. During the chubby Michael years, I had been to the doctor various times regarding my high blood pressure. It hadn't been at a level that required medication but was something they would comment on at every appointment. This, combined with being a white coat syndrome sufferer, had me fearing that the medical certificate would be a no go. However, with Paris a firm Olympic city, I had to give it a go. As it transpired, my blood pressure was fine and the certificate was signed with no problem. I guess the running had not only stopped me outgrowing my clothes but also helped with my overall health. Double bonus.

Forms in hand, I set off to Paris on the Eurostar. As all UK residents know, a train journey is not the same unless you stock up on a train picnic from M&S Simply Food. Typically, I find that I have eaten said picnic just as the train is pulling out of the station, even if it is only ten in the morning. Today was no exception to this trend. I did manage to resist a little before reaching for my yoghurt snack, only to find it had split inside my race bag. Brilliant. On the bright side, I suppose it meant that my headphones (and in turn my ears) would smell nicely of Madagascan vanilla all the way round the race the next day.

Upon my arrival in Paris, I decided to head straight to the race expo before checking into my hotel so that I could then do all the necessary race preparation and then relax before a nice dinner with a friend. The metro ride to packet pickup started with a busker serenading us with the French sounds of the accordion, making me definitely feel that I had arrived in Paris. It always amuses me that the accordion is the adopted instrument of many a busker in metro stations the world over but I am yet to see one on the London Underground. Perhaps a gap in the market for those budding musicians out there? A quick change of metro line altered the street entertainment somewhat, to a teenager dancing like Michael Jackson to "Beat It", complete with sequined jacket and hat. I am not sure which of the two impressed me most. It was a tough choice.

It has to be said that the walk from the metro to the registration tent certainly helped loosen the muscles and work up an appetite, for it was the longest walk I have ever endured to pick up a race number. I calculated about twenty-three minutes. Due to my performance in Barcelona, I was upgraded to the first start wave, which was a bonus and left me excited for the race the next day.

I checked into my hotel and went through my pre-race preparation of reading the race leaflet and setting out my clothes for the next day. The checklist in the race book kindly said to remember to apply anti-chafe cream and, if necessary, "apply two plasters to your tits". Cue me laughing like an immature young teenager. At dinner, I stocked up on a ridiculous amount of bread, cheese, and pasta. To my regret, the only missing part of my nourishment was some lovely French red wine.

Race morning was crisp but sporting a perfect blue sky, much like the weather the week before in Rome. It made me excited to get out there and run. I had not been in a race this large for quite some time. Having forty thousand runners causes a lot of excitement and body heat to benefit from at the start line, and before I knew it, 10 a.m. struck and the start gun fired. The race began in Chateau de Vincennes, which, despite my being a regular in Paris, I had never visited. It was a splendid place to start, the first five to seven kilometres through the adjacent park a perfect way to begin a Sunday morning run. Even though I was in the first start wave, I had not experienced such a crowding of people for the first kilometre in a long time. It made it difficult to build up to my usual pace, but it didn't actually worry me. Today I was just interested in doing the run and taking in the sights. The goal of another PB was not on the agenda.

Exiting the park, we hit the streets of Paris and the first glimpse of the Seine and Notre Dame was welcomed, adding much fuel to the fire of speeding on through to the end. As we passed each kilometre marker, I realized I was making good progress and had managed to maintain a good pace despite not following a pacemaker as I had done three weeks earlier in Barcelona. The crowds and fellow runners helped me arrive home in a time of one hour, twenty minutes, and fifty-two seconds, placing me 297th out of 37,500, a result with which I was extremely happy.

Finishing back at the chateau, the race organisers were offering free massages to runners. I have never taken this offer up in other races, but since this was such a nice setting, I decided to give it a go. It was certainly well worth it and something I would like to do again should the offer arise. My feet and legs were grateful afterwards. The only embarrassing part was having to remove my socks and publicly display my dreadful runners' feet (complete with black toenails) to the man performing the massage. He didn't seem to acknowledge them and carried on as normal. Perhaps he saw this all the time – or was it that he just wanted to get the unenviable task of touching my feet over and done with?

Having a few hours before my train home, I decided to celebrate the run with a croque madame for lunch and a wonderful walk through the Père Lachaise Cemetery. Those who have been to the cemetery surely appreciate both its beauty and size. Simply searching for Edith Piaf's and Oscar Wilde's graves, I think I added about another five kilometres to the distance I ran that morning, but it was absolutely worth it. After locating the graves, it was then back to London, feeling satisfied with another city run and done. Also, who knew that I would have the talent to finish a chapter with a rhyming couplet?

Target cities: 23
Completed: 8

Chapter 11

Antwerp – The Diamond City

Olympic year: 1920
Antwerp Olympic fact: It was the first time the
Olympic flag made an appearance.

Next up: Belgium.

Belgium is a country that is close to my heart, having lived there for five years. Yet the country still seems to hold quite a bland reputation with those who have not been – and regretfully even to some who have. I disagree with all those who sit in either camp. It's a great place to visit.

I was excited to be heading back there to see some of the old haunts, visit friends, eat chocolate, and have some of the beer, including the girly but tasty cherry beer Kriek.

The previous year, I had done the Brussels twenty-kilometre race in one hour and twenty-three minutes, thoroughly enjoying running past places that I recognized from childhood, so I knew that I would feel the same running in another Belgian city. Antwerp was also where my sister was born. Hats off to my parents for arranging for both of their children to be born in an Olympic city. I was making the trip to Antwerp for the weekend with my mother, sister, and new niece. She was only four months old, and it was to be her first trip abroad. It was also the first time that I would be the person on the plane with the screaming child. I was fully prepared for people to see me in the airport with her and comment how cute she was whilst secretly thinking, *please don't be seated next to me.*

At London City Airport, I tried to check in for the flight and was told to report to the information desk. This is never a good sign. With my sister and niece checking in without an issue, I thought perhaps it would not be a major problem; however, I was firmly told that due to a possible weight restriction on the aircraft, I would not be able to check in at this time and may not be able to fly. I knew I hadn't been that careful with what I had been eating recently, but surely I was not going to be the issue that caused a plane not to be able to take off due to my weight? Those chubby Michael days were behind me, no? But it seemed not. Due to the direction in which the small aircraft was to take off, a lighter load was required; I had to wait to see if my mother and I would be accepted. *At least there's another flight to Antwerp an hour later,* I thought. But I was told it was already full.

"So how will you be getting me to Belgium if I don't get the original flight?" I asked.

"Not an issue," came the reply. "We will fly you to Rotterdam and then drive you to Antwerp."

What kind of solution was that? Were they not aware that Rotterdam was outside the Belgian border?

Fortunately, the Gods were playing in my favour and both my mother and I were accepted on the flight. All four of us were on our way. Running to the gate to board the plane, I quickly texted Steven to regale the story (in a shortened version), and whilst trying to say I had a mini-strop at the information desk, auto correct had me saying, "After a little strip at the information desk, we are now on the flight." I have to say that during the wait to find out if we were going to be able to fly, I quite happily would have stripped to get us all on the same flight, and if I had to hazard a guess at the sexuality of the male manager who was in charge of the situation, I have a feeling that this method would perhaps have worked had we needed it.

The weekend was spent catching up with old friends, some of whom I had not seen since I was fifteen, which was a full seventeen years early, as well as visiting some of the both famous and not-so-famous fantastic sights in and around Antwerp, like the Grote Markt, Leonidas chocolate shops, my Dad's old office, and my old house.

The run was a ten-mile run, which was a slightly odd distance for a run on the continent. My only experience of a ten-mile event was the Great South Run in Portsmouth. I had competed in that in 2011 and 2012, with times of one hour, five minutes, and fifty-five seconds and one hour, two minutes, and twenty-two seconds, respectively. I enjoyed the Great South Run, but because it takes place on the coast in the UK in late October, it makes the waiting in the cold for the start gun a challenge in itself. Therefore, this run being in April, I was hoping for a more temperate start and possibly another slightly quicker time.

The week before the run, the Boston Marathon had taken place but had fallen victim to a terrorist attack. Two bombs were detonated at the finish line, which killed three people and severely injured hundreds of others. Scarily, the incident resonated with the theme of the film *Four Lions*, and with the London Marathon due to take place the same day as my Antwerp run, I couldn't help but feel sad for those who had lost their lives in Boston. I wondered why anyone would want to hurt people who were simply running and, in many cases, raising money for worthwhile charities. At the start of the Antwerp run, a thirty-second silence was held to reflect on the tragedy that had happened in Boston just six days earlier.

Despite this, the DJ then managed to create an excited crowd of twenty-five thousand runners. The run started, but within a few hundred metres, I was worried it was all going to tits up, a la Barcelona style. A fellow runner ahead of me dropped his headphones, and rather than accept that they were gone turned round and started running back into a headwind of twenty-five thousand runners to retrieve them. Fool. That's the kindest word I can find in my vocabulary to describe him. It was definitely not one of his best ideas. Fortunately, I spotted him in time to swerve and miss him.

Carrying on, I started to feel something that I was definitely not used to. It was a stitch. I couldn't work out why, as I had not overloaded on food beforehand. It was quite a surprise to me. I thought the pain would subside after a few hundred metres, but it didn't. It carried on for around two and a half kilometres. I knew that I would eventually be able to run it out and was determined not to stop running at any point until I won the battle.

Battle won, I could then enjoy the run and take in the main sights – some cobbled streets and a couple of road tunnels under the river – which was fun when going downhill, but the long slow incline to come out of them was less appealing. Seeing the light at the end of the tunnel (literally) was a joy, but it still took an age to arrive.

I finished the race in one hour, two minutes, and fifteen seconds, which was just inside my PB for that distance by five seconds, placing me 225th. It was the end to another successful Olympic challenge, and I rounded it off with a few Belgian beers and chocolate.

Target cities: 23
Completed: 9

Chapter 12

Berlin – Meet Her at the Love Parade

Olympic years: 1916 and 1936
Berlin Olympic Fact: 1936 was the first time the now traditional torch relay took place, carrying the flame from Olympia (the setting of the ancient Olympic Games) in Greece to Berlin.

Willkommen, Bievenue, Welcome im Cabaret, au Cabaret, to Cabaret!

I love Berlin, and a fifth visit to this city was most welcome, as per the above rather camp greeting. It's a fascinating city, very rich in history and, as the current mayor put it, "poor but sexy".

To jazz up my challenge, I had signed up for the Big Berlin running weekend, which included a ten-kilometre race, a half marathon, and a twenty-five-kilometre race. I had opted for the latter length because I thought it may keep the blog a little more interesting.

Training had been along the lines of my usual routine, and it was only two weeks before the run that it dawned on me that twenty-five kilometres was actually quite a bit farther than my usual ten thousand kilometres or even half marathon. Slight panic. But after a short word with myself, I decided I could definitely make it round the course and that I wasn't going to concentrate on achieving a particular time. Since it was the only time I had been in a race of this length, it was guaranteed to be a personal best, no matter what the result.

It was the May bank holiday in the UK, which allowed me to go to Berlin for three nights and enjoy a much more relaxed pace than my usual weekend jaunt to do the previous races earlier in the challenge. As per usual, I spent the first day registering for the event, taking in the sights a la open-top bus, and buying a flag for my intended finishing photo.

Soon Sunday rolled around and it was time to head to the Olympic stadium for the start of the race. Very thoughtful for the race organisers to arrange for the run to both start and end on the actual Olympic race track itself. A perfect fit for this chapter of the book and my challenge.

It was a very hot day, which I had been prepared for by packing a vest top to run in so I would hopefully not dehydrate part way round the course. The atmosphere at the start was great, and with all three races starting at the same point at the same time, it was great to see such a mix of participants ready for challenges of all different kinds. I was put in the first start wave, and this was the first time in any event that I was so close to the front that I actually saw the elite runners coming out and lining up on the start line. It made me feel excited for the hour or two ahead. In what felt like an appropriate Europop moment, they played "The Final Countdown" by Europe in the last minute before the start. Almost made me feel I was in a local German discotheque, which I feel are some of the best discos around.

The start gun sounded, and within a few seconds, I was off listening to my party pop playlist again. The route was rather flat and went past many of the top attractions, including the Brandenburg Gate. It was a fantastic course and a wonderful way to see the city again.

After the ten-kilometre and half marathon runners split off from the twenty-five-kilometre route, I found myself essentially running alone. The leaders were pretty far ahead of me, and I didn't seem to have any other competitors close behind me either – a lonely place to be so I shed a little tear. Just kidding. Seriously, though, it did almost felt as if I had the city streets to myself, bar some supporters along the sidelines, which was brilliant. One of my favourite moments of the race was at about eight kilometres. I turned the corner and was on the long street (Unter den Linden) that leads up to the Victory Column, where the Love Parade used to take place. I had always wanted to go to Love Parade but never made it before the event was stopped. What gave me a buzz on the run was that as soon as the column was in sight, "Meet her at the Love Parade" came on to my playlist. How random is that? Filled with excitement about this, I think I ran one of the quickest kilometres of the day (and my life, for that matter). A few minutes later, with my adrenaline in check, I was back to a normal pace.

I can't deny that the BIG 25 is a long race, and it took a lot of mental preparation and focus to not get distracted by how far it actually was to the end. However, the Olympic stadium was soon in sight, so I knew we were on the home stretch. I have to say, though, that those last two kilometres were pretty hard, especially as you have to circumnavigate the entire stadium knowing that just inside is the finish line. Despite the torture of knowing it was so close, it really did feel amazing to go into the tunnel into the stadium and hear the crowd on the other side when we hit the track. It was a real treat of a way to end a race, second only to the marathon in Athens.

Upon crossing the finish line, I knew I had done well but wasn't expecting this result:

Time: one hour, thirty-six minutes, and fifty-seven seconds

Overall place: twenty-first

Men's place: fifteenth

Age group (male – thirty) place: second

I was over the moon – and every planet in fact.

I celebrated that afternoon with a large amount of food and a fro-yo, followed by lying on the man-made "Charlie's Beach", just by Checkpoint Charlie, with a few Coronas in the scorching sunshine. A brilliant day.

Perhaps the next day would require a little rest? Don't be silly. Laura and I were up early for a five-hour bike tour around the former East Berlin. It was another excellent day and kept my muscles loose as well as cleared the head after the few too many cocktails the night before. On the flight home, I was happy with such a fun weekend in a great city.

I came home to the following email from my running coach:

> *Top run, just seen results and shows that you ran very close to your half marathon PB [and] then continued at a very similar pace (ten seconds per mile slower by my calculations) for a further 3.9 kilometres, so that's fine stuff. It's a big haul, so do allow recovery. Bet you didn't expect to come in fifteenth as you stood on the start line!*

With such encouragement like that, plus being asked if I was a professional runner by the man next to me on the plane, I was filled with pride and knew it would be tough to get to sleep that night, but it was time for bed, as a six-mile training run beckoned the next morning before work.

Target cities: 23
Completed: 10

Chapter 13

Amsterdam – A Splash, No Hash

Olympic year: 1928
Amsterdam Olympic fact: For the duration of
the games, many of the athletes were housed
in the ships that brought them to the city.

Amsterdam is a popular city break offering art, history, canals, coffee shops, and the infamous red-light district. I have been a visitor to the city on numerous occasions, taking in some of the above. I was thrilled to be back.

With it being only a short hop away from London, it always makes me think that I should be a more frequent visitor, and every time I swear to myself that I won't wait so long before I next walk on Dutch soil.

For my next Olympic event, I was forced to opt for a little bit of a gear change when I read that the ten-mile race that the city puts on was to land on the same weekend as the Beijing triathlon, which I was already entered into as my next Olympic city. After a few searches online, I stumbled across the Amsterdam City Swim, which was to take place just a couple of weeks prior to the run I had been banking on. The inaugural year for the event was 2012, and the 1.5-kilometre swim in the city's extensive one hundred kilometres of canals seemed to have gone swimmingly (pun again intended); even the crown princess had taken part. Given that I had been training for the swimming portion of my triathlons, I thought it would be perfect timing to enter the swim. The princess that took part the previous year was now actually the queen of the Netherlands, so this could also be the one and only time I could get to swim with a real live queen.

Researching a little about the swimming happenings during the actual Amsterdam Olympics in 1928, it seems that Johnny Weissmuller won two gold medals and then later on went on to appear in the Tarzan films. That was it, then. A swimming challenge it was to be (hopefully followed up by offers from Hollywood).

I entered the race and pledged to raise funds for the nominated charity ALS (for the illness commonly known as Lou Gehrig's disease), knowing I could also take on a lifestyle change by adopting people's advice of not swallowing during the race itself. Fundraising was going well, and I was set to head out to Amsterdam when I had a look at the joining instructions again. Seemingly, it appeared that the distance of the race had increased from 1,500 to 2,013 metres. I see what they did there with the year (it being 2013), but an extra 500 metres in a swim race is quite a difference as opposed to just adding it on to a run! Oh well. No time for moaning. I was sure I could make it, and if I needed to hang on to the legs of the queen in front of me, then so be it. I am sure I would be able to find one in Amsterdam, even if it was not the actual queen. After all, this city holds its gay pride parade on the canal instead of the streets. Perhaps a few stray drag queens may still be lingering in the water after this year's parade to help me along?

The whole of the night before the swim, I had been awakened to the sound of torrential rain, which didn't worry me so much for my own sake (after all, I was going to be wet anyway) but for the spectators who would either have to brave the elements or take hold of their senses and simply not support the swimmers. However, after breakfast the sun miraculously came out and helped create an electric atmosphere at the start area. I was nervous but excited and pleased to be in the second wave of starters so that I didn't have to hang around too long. The professionals were set off by the firing of a loud canon from a ship in the dock. Shortly afterwards, I jumped into the canals and was on my way too.

The first section of the swim was in more open water, so it felt it was taking ages to reach the first bridge. Once there, though, we were into the smaller canals of the city and there were supporters everywhere. It was fantastic to see so many people standing and sitting on the bridges, streets, and houseboats shouting their support. I felt OK and was going at a good pace, and not too long into the race, I passed the one-thousand-metre buoy. Pleased as punch to be halfway, I carried on and thoroughly enjoyed every remaining metre. As I drew closer to the end, I even found the energy to switch onto my back as I went under bridges and give the crowd above me a wave, doing a small dive to rival even the best of the cetaceans in Sea World.

At the end, I sat on the dock for a few minutes to gather my breath. Exiting the canal, my feet were a little wobbly, but in the best ending to an event, they gave you a brand-new dressing gown, flip-flops, a banana, and a Red Bull equivalent called Hard Water to revitalize you. Amaze.

I finished the swim in a time of thirty-seven minutes and thirty-one seconds, placing me 122nd out of 1,772 swimmers, which I was pleased with. Walking back to the start line, various members of the public stopped me in the street to congratulate me, which made me feel important and celeb-like. Top tip for those entering a swimming race, though, is to remember to pack underwear in your kit bag; otherwise, you will have to spend the rest of the day going commando.

I loved every second of this event, and I hope to be back one day to take part again.

Target cities: 23
Completed: 11

P.S. I only swallowed twice, and there was still no sign of the queen ...

Chapter 14

Beijing – Lost in the Suburbs

Olympic year: 2008
Beijing Olympic fact: Michael Phelps won eight gold
medals during the games, making him the only
athlete to win that many in a single Olympics.

In June 2012, I luckily gained a place in the Escape from Alcatraz Triathlon in San Francisco. I had heard about this event a few years before and thought that it sounded unlike any other triathlon on Earth. It is described as "a one-and-a-half-mile swim through frigid waters from Alcatraz Island to shore, a gruelling eighteen-mile bike race, and a demanding eight-mile run through the rugged trails of Golden Gate National Recreation Area." It sounded tough, and even my Dad's comment of "You are aware why that prison is so famous; nobody ever escaped" didn't deter me from entering the lottery to gain a place. I half didn't expect to get a spot, so when the email came through saying I had, and that I had only a short time to confirm my place and pay the entry fee, I was a little unsure of what to do. I thought about it for a few minutes, asked my colleagues sitting around me, took their encouragement, grew a pair, and paid my entry fee.

I had done enough training for the triathlon. However, for the four months prior to the event, my Dad had been in hospital, which had meant lots of time away from home visiting him – thus my final preparation for the trip had not been up to my usual standard (ignoring my Barcelona packing blip.)

I had planned to take my bike with me, as the airline I was travelling with allowed you to take it for free as long as it was in a bike box. I thought this was perfect, and the day before heading out to San Francisco, I went to pick up a bike box from my local bike shop. Only when seeing it did I fully understand that you have to dismantle the bike partially to fit it in and make it travel ready. Being a clueless bike mechanic, I knew this was not an option, as there would be no way I could put it back together and make it race safe. So on the train that night, I was trying to rent a bike in San Francisco via a mobile phone for pick up the next day. Slightly worried that no sites I checked would have availability, I eventually found one that did, and despite it not being a road racer, it had two wheels (and a bag version of a basket on the front), so it was good enough for me.

I arrived in San Francisco excited for the event, planning to go for a swim in the bay to try out my brand-new wetsuit and to see how genuinely cold the bay water was. Was it really going to be "frigid", as they said? I went down to the beach before breakfast, suited up, and waded into the water. The verdict? The bay water is absolutely fucking freezing. I made it about two minutes in the water (without even putting my face in) before jumping out of the water shivering and thus starting what turned out to be a rather stressful but in hindsight a funny day. Post-swim (well, two-second dip) I went for breakfast, where my friends tried to reassure me that it would all be fine on the day. I agreed and went to register for the event.

All went OK at registration, and I went back for a swim in the bay. I brought my wetsuit down to the beach, and as I was zipping it up, I heard an unhealthy ripping sound. Panicked, I took it back off and saw that the entire zip had come away at the back. Trauma.

How could this happen to a brand-new suit and less than twenty-four hours prior to race start! A fellow competitor overheard my unsavoury language and said that sometimes you can swim with rips in wetsuits. He then saw mine and quickly retracted the statement, pointing me in the direction of a shop that sold wetsuits.

At the shop, whilst looking like the most unprepared triathlete ever, I also invested in a wetsuit cap and socks; anything to keep me from re-enacting the end of *Titanic* seemed like money well spent to me. I then went back to the beach for the third time that day and tried swimming. It went well. I was warm enough and could put my face in the water, so I felt much more ready for the next day.

The triathlon itself was amazing. Not only was it set in a beautiful city but also it feel quite cool to be one of a handful of people to be able to say that I have escaped from Alcatraz. At the end of the race, we got given the usual pamphlets for other events we may be interested in, and within that was the promotion for the inaugural Beijing International Triathlon that was to take place later that year. So when it came to searching for what I should do in Beijing, the decision was clear. Another triathlon it was. This time I booked my bike hire well in advance. I also felt a little more prepared for this trip because I was reassured that my trusty wetsuit purchased in San Francisco had seen me through not only the escape triathlon but the Amsterdam City Swim.

I arrived in Beijing a few days prior to the event in order to adjust to the time difference, but mainly to explore this wonderful city. I took a bike tour around the old city, seeing amazing temples and lunching with a local family in their house, all with the knowledge that it was a little bit of training for the triathlon too. The city is packed with people, culture, aromas (including gruel which the restaurant opposite our hotel was kindly serving), and energy. I loved it from the start. To get further into the mood for my challenge, I went up to the Olympic park to see the fantastic Bird's Nest Stadium and Water Cube aquatic centre, coming away excited and with some cuddly toys in the shape of the 2008 Olympic mascots for my niece (and me).

The transport system in Beijing is excellent, and we made our way around the city on the extensive underground. Similar to London, they had pre-paid cards which you swiped to get in and out of the gates. Now, being a local in London, I have been known to occasionally get a little frustrated with tourists when they seem to struggle with the concept of touching your card on the reader and then keep on walking through the gate. It's not that hard, people! To my horror, I soon became one of these tourists in Beijing when on the way back from the Olympic park, my ticket wouldn't let me out. I couldn't understand it as I stood there and the lights firmly stayed on red. Pushing back through the crowd to a ticket inspector, he shook his head and implied I needed to buy a new ticket. Not sure why and not wanting to hold up locals anymore, I did so and was allowed out of the station and onto the street (in the non-prostitute kind of way). It wasn't until we got back to the hotel that I took the room key out of my pocket and swiped it to get into our room. This wasn't working either. How could this be? Maybe it just wasn't my day? But no. Looking at the room key, I realized I was trying to get into the room with my metro ticket and had therefore been trying to exit the metro with my room key. What a moron. No wonder it didn't work. I had to lap up the shame and go down to reception to explain that somewhere on the Beijing underground was my room key and I needed a new one. Oops.

The triathlon itself was to be held around Qing Long Lake Park, which lies about thirty-five kilometres outside the city itself. On arrival at the hotel, there was a good atmosphere, as most triathletes were staying at the official hotel. I was 90 per cent excited about the event and kept about 10 per cent of my energy in the format of nerves, as I was a tiny bit worried that my bike was not going to turn up as I was hoping it would.

I checked into the hotel and then went to find the bike hire man. He was there with a rack load of road racers. This was great – all working as I had planned. He ticked my name off and got a bike out for me, but then he did worry me slightly when he asked if I had brought my own peddles. WTF? Do people really do that? Perhaps they do, but I certainly didn't. That aside, he took some off another bike and attached them to mine. That done, I was now race ready.

The race registration and bike rack was down at the lake, which was about seven kilometres down the road from the hotel. The seven-kilometre ride down there would do me well, as I had never actually ridden a racer before, so it would be good practice as well as get me to the lake. The instructions seemed too simple: turn right, then right again, and go straight until you reach the lake. I thought I had done exactly that, but clearly not, as I carried on straight until I reached the entrance to the motorway, not quite the quiet surroundings of a lake. I luckily had the map written in Chinese so I could stop various people to ask for directions. They were all very helpful, but somehow I ended up lost in many suburban villages for quite some time, making me start to think that I may actually miss the athletes meeting I needed to attend. Having made many local friends along the way, I made it to the race expo, covering an estimated fifteen kilometres instead of the original planned seven kilometres. After regaling the story to my friend Claire, who was on the trip with me, she chuckled and told me that had it been her, she would have been crying, which made me laugh in return.

The Beijing International Triathlon was set up to act as a qualifier for the Escape from Alcatraz Triathlon, thus it followed a similar format in that it was a tough course and only the first person from each age category would get a place in the event the following summer. The swim was a 1.5-kilometre clockwise lap of the lake. Starting very early allowed me to be at the lake for sunrise, which was a beautiful sight and made the 4 a.m. alarm worthwhile. The various waves were separated by age, so I wasn't far behind the elites in terms of start time – but of course a long way behind them in the end.

The bike ride was forty kilometres and was partially flat but did involve cycling up a mountain which offered spectacular views of the surrounding area, which was challenging, to say the least. Coming down the mountain, we then went through some villages (one of which I am sure I had visited the prior day on my accidental detour), which was fun because I wasn't used to these types of events. All the villagers were outside their houses cheering, waving, and taking photos with their phones. It created a lovely atmosphere and gave me a much-needed boost to complete the mileage of the ride.

The run was a ten-kilometre off-road run. I was pretty comfortable throughout the run, even when it came to the steps. One shock I did have was that I got a terrible cramp in my inner thigh (presumably delayed from the cycle), which forced me to stop for around forty seconds or so. This had never happened to me before, and I was worried about how long it would last and what would it mean as far as finishing the race. A fellow competitor saw my troubles and told me to slap my inner thigh and it would go. Always willing to try anything I spanked myself (good fun) and was shortly on my way cramp-free.

Crossing the finish line was great (especially because they read out your name as you approached the finish), and I was pleased to have completed the race. My results were broken down as follows:

Overall place: 135th out of 377
Division place: 29th out of 73
Gender place: 125th out of 334
Overall time: Two hours and fifty-seven minutes

Swim (1.5 kilometre): Twenty-seven minutes and thirty-three seconds

Bike (forty kilometres): one hour, thirty-eight minutes, and thirty seconds

Run (ten kilometres): forty-one minutes and fifty-nine seconds

I was pleased with this, for it was a tough race. It also included an extra six-hundred-meter run from the swim exit to transition, which adds on a little time to the usual triathlon.

The swim and run were decent times. I was actually twentieth overall for the run, second for my division, and forty-fourth overall for the swim, sixth for my division, but my bike ride really let me down. To be honest, I didn't train as much on the bike as I probably should have, but in my defence, I am still rather nervous since a bike accident back in 2007, which puts me off cycling around the busy streets of London. As I said, this cycle involved heading up a mountain, but even on the downhill parts, I was just too nervous to freewheel. I tell myself that this is why almost everyone (including someone on a fold-up Brompton commuter bike) overtook me. I hold no shame for this.

Post-race I headed back to central Beijing giving a wide berth to the restaurant by our hotel that was proudly advertising they served gruel. Instead I enjoyed Peking duck, Tsingtao beer, and a trek along the Great Wall. A fantastic way to finish off a wonderful trip and a completely enjoyable race. No qualification for me for the Escape from Alcatraz the next year, but perhaps that was just as well since my bank balance may cry even more than it already is with all these Olympic events to keep up with.

Target: 23
Completed: 12

Chapter 15

Munich – Do I Risk a Beer?

Olympic year: 1972
Munich Olympic fact: The games were interrupted when eight Palestinian terrorists broke into the athletes' village and shot dead two of the Israeli team and kidnapped a further nine. All the hostages, five of the terrorists, and one police officer were killed in a gunfight later the same day. Definitely the darkest moment in Olympics history.

It dawned on me that I was over halfway to completing my challenge. How did that happen? It was now truly starting to feel as if I could achieve it – and that other people will believe I can too. To begin with, when I told some people about it, I could sense that they thought it was unachievable and that I would do one or two races and then give up. I am more determined than ever now to get through it.

So on to city number thirteen. Unlucky for some? A little weekend jaunt to Munich beckoned, and the half marathon fell perfectly in October. Sadly (despite the name suggesting otherwise), the Oktoberfest actually takes place in September, which meant there would be no overindulging on beer and full chickens for me this time. The first time I visited Munich was purely for said beer festival, and I have to say for the moments I remember, I very much enjoyed the city. It is quite famous amongst my friends and colleagues that I never suffer from hangovers. Despite how hammered I get, I still feel OK the next day and can continue with whatever the day's plans hold. However, having consumed six litres of beer in one day at the Oktoberfest, danced on tables, eaten copious amounts of meat, ridden roller coasters, and spouted utter crap to my friend (and strangers), I went to bed with the thought that I would be perfectly fine in the morning for our day trip to Neuschwanstein Castle, farther south in Germany. Big fat no. I awoke with a feeling that was all too peculiar to me. A little nausea?

I ignored it, showered, dressed, and went downstairs to check in online for my flight later than night. But all of a sudden, the sick feeling was too great for me to handle. I went to run up to my room, only to discover that I had forgotten my key and could not even operate the lift without the use of said key. Thus I was stuck in the lobby. What to do? I scurried outside the hotel but could no longer refrain and was sick into a plant pot outside our lovely four-star hotel. Talk about looking like a proper Brit abroad on Booze Britain. The shame.

I returned to my room, brushed my teeth, and then felt ready for the day. From start to finish, I calculated that my hangover had lasted twenty-three minutes. I commented to my friend Laura that I knew exactly how she felt now when she muttered the words "I feel rough", only to receive a response that I most certainly did not and only once I had felt like that for three days would I understand other people's pain and reality of a hangover.

So heading out to Munich for the half marathon, it was a good thing that the Oktoberfest had already been and gone and that I adopted a no-drinking policy for the night before any sporting event. I was obviously staying in a different hotel to the one where the above happened, which was necessary to avoid being recognised, especially as it was one of the official sponsor hotels of the race weekend. I had already decided to take it easy in the race since it would be my third half marathon in as many weeks. In addition, the race the week before in Cardiff was a new personal best of one hour, nineteen minutes, and twenty-two seconds. Pleased to now be a sub-one-hour-and-twenty-minute runner, I thought I was allowed to simply enjoy this race and not try to break any records, be them Olympic or my own.

Arriving in Munich, it was a little chilly and rather cloudy. I had been told it was going to be snowing before my arrival but wasn't able to see a flake anywhere. I had packed spikes to wear on my trainers for the run in the snow, but I clearly wasn't going to need them. I spent the day visiting the Dachau concentration camp, which is quite a harrowing but interesting way to spend a day, quite different from my usual bus tour. Whilst sites like this are not enjoyable as such, I would definitely encourage visitors to the city to put it on their to-do list, as I believe it's important that we don't forget what the people sent to these camps went through. The most difficult part of the visit for me was seeing the crematorium and gas chamber at the same time the local church bells were ringing. It was an odd feeling.

After an intense day, I went to register for my event at the Olympic park and had a currywurst afterwards on the way back to my hotel. The Olympic stadium is one of the most unusual ones I have seen, so I was super excited to be getting to finish the race inside it the following day. Race day included a marathon, half marathon, and ten kilometres, so athletes were everywhere on the streets and metro. The half marathon was not starting until 2 p.m., which allowed me to have a little lie-in and even manage breakfast and lunch before a race, which is a rarity!

Arriving at the start, I noted that there was a good atmosphere. I made my way to the front runners to line up for the gun. The countdown was pretty exciting to hear in German: "Zehn, neun, acht, sieben, sechs, funf, vier, drei, zwei, ein" – and we were off!

The course took us through the city, past many historical buildings (including one Hitler made one of his last addresses from) and under the spectacular arch in the centre of town. Despite not wanting a

PB, I did still look at my watch each kilometre marker to ensure I was under my target of one hour and twenty-five minutes, remaining happy when I saw that I was. I enjoyed the race and not having the pressure of beating my time from the week before, which allowed me to just relax and run. At around eight kilometres, we started to overtake the last of the marathon runners, which was a weird feeling, as I couldn't help but think of what must be going through their minds. I am certain that the names they had for those of us passing them were not printable or complimentary.

As I arrived at the Olympic park, I took off my headphones to take in the atmosphere. The DJ was playing some absolute *tunes*! It was brilliant. One lap of the track and I was home in a time of one hour, twenty-three minutes, and forty-eight seconds, making me fifty-third (eleventh for my age group) out of 6,462. I was pleased and especially so with the medal since it was shaped like a heart, much like the gingerbread that is sold everywhere in town. There was time for me to have some photos taken in the stadium with my medal and newly acquired Bavarian flag before heading for a shower to clear my face of the ridiculous amount of salt that it had created (proof that although I run a lot, it still requires effort to complete a half marathon in that time). One of my pet peeves is when people say, "Oh, it's easy for you to run a half marathon since you do it all the time." Um, no. It's still tough, but I enjoy it. If I make it look easy, then that's an achievement, but let me reassure you it's not. A nice note from my running coach after the event:

> *Amongst the highly travelled people I coach, I think you are doing the most country hopping! Good that you could do mid eighty-three minutes and still feel that it was "taking it easy"!*

So with an event in Munich under my belt, that meant that I had now completed all of my European Olympic cities (unless we include Moscow in Europe, which I am never sure if we do or not. Russia are in the Eurovision Song Contest, which indicates yes, but then the country does stretch across to Asia, so where Moscow lies,

I am unsure). That aside, it meant that from now on, all my events would require more planning and investment in terms of travel time. Nevertheless, I was looking forward to it. Bring it on!

Target: 23
Completed: 13

P.S. I did have a stein of beer on the evening of the race but refrained from having six like last time. The plant pots in the hotel were all safe this time.

Chapter 16

Montreal – Running with a Chilly Willy

Olympic year: 1976
Montreal Olympic fact: It was the first time a perfect
ten had been awarded in gymnastics.

Each year I had wanted to compete in a slightly unusual run in addition to the Olympic ones. In January 2013, I took part in the Polar Night Half Marathon. The run takes place in Tromso in Norway, which lies seventy degrees north, within the Arctic Circle. Being in January snow was guaranteed, and it would be dark at the start time of three pm since there is roughly only one to two hours of daylight per day at this time of year in the region. A chance sighting of the Northern Lights was also a maybe, so it sounded as if it met my criteria of being unusual.

I arrived in Tromso on my own and was pleasantly surprised at how mild the weather was (in comparison to what I expected). On the first night, there was a welcome pasta party at the local aquarium, and I went to the party to enjoy my bowl of reindeer pasta and then had a look around the aquarium, which was fun. I wasn't sure how many people were taking part but I was definitely expecting more than the handful of people who were there for the party and the pre-race briefing. It couldn't have been more than sixty. The race director welcomed us to the region and told us about the route, start times, and so forth. He left us with one bit of advice: "Since it has been warm during the day [one to two degrees centigrade] but then dropping below zero at night, it means that the snow is melting and then turning to ice by the morning. With that in mind, I suggest you run with spikes on your shoes."

OMG. I had read the joining instructions, which specifically said that spikes were not needed. I had a pair of trainers that had extra grip but no spikes. Coming to terms with the fact that I would need some local advice on how to resolve this situation, I reluctantly shared my plight with the race director. He was very friendly and didn't at all make me feel like the idiot I was. He told me the name of a shop in town that I could go to prior to the race to buy some.

When race morning arrived, I skidded my way to the shop and purchased one of the few remaining pairs of spikes. To try them out, I put them straight on and walked back to my hotel. A success. No slips or sliding at all. I got ready for the race in my many (and I mean *many*) layers, hat, gloves, and new spikes and then headed down to the start area on the main street. I had a bit of time, so I went for a spot of lunch in a lovely quiet cafe. Thirty minutes before the start I went out to the start line, where there were flamethrowers lighting up the already dark sky. I spotted a few runners in just shorts and T-shirts and immediately thought how unprepared they were not to be wrapped up like me.

Roll forward five kilometres into the race and the shoe (complete with spikes) was firmly on the other foot. I was boiling and had to put up with feeling like an oven. The spikes certainly did the trick, although after sixteen kilometres they did begin to rub on my little toes – so much so that when I returned to the hotel, I was a little nervous to take off my trainers in case my socks were covered with blood. It turns out this was me just being a little dramatic. Not one drop of blood was shed.

I thoroughly enjoyed the run and having the route lit by candlelight in the snow was beautiful. Sadly, the Northern Lights didn't make an appearance, and despite taking a wrong turn and running up a very steep hill (being chased by the marshal to bring me back), I finished the race in one hour, twenty-seven minutes, and nineteen seconds, which placed me sixth in my age category. In total, there were around nine hundred competitors (so much more than had been at the party the night before).

So why am I telling you about a run in Norway that was not even in a Winter Olympics city? When it came to researching what event to do in Montreal, I had been looking for half marathons and stumbled across one called the Hypothermic Half Marathon. What the fuck was that? Upon research, I read that it was of course a half marathon in the city – but in February. So in short, it would be covered in snow and absolutely freezing. To keep you, my dear reader, interested and turning to another page, I will tell you that I entered the race. After all, I had completed a run in the snow before, and I hoped this would be a way to keep my Olympic challenge fresh (literally) and interesting to read about. The entry fee didn't include a willy warmer, but it did include a hat and gloves; therefore, I could likely keep hypothermia at bay.

Arriving in Montreal, it was about minus fifteen degrees centigrade. Quite chilly.

I spent the first couple of days seeing the city (stopping in numerous coffee shops for a warm drink of any kind), ice-skating on the frozen lake, and even managing to find an outdoor spa on a boat on the river to relax and warm my muscles before the big event.

At race packet pickup the day before the race, when I handed over my passport as ID, the organisers were quite shocked. It said I was Michael Long from London, which they had assumed would be London in Ontario (i.e., still in Canada), so when they saw a British passport and I confirmed that I had indeed travelled all the way from London, England, to compete in the race, they were astounded. Clearly, this race didn't attract too many international runners then.

It actually made me feel like a little bit of a celebrity for a second, before they moved on to the next person in line.

When race day came around, it was minus eleven degrees. I dressed (the exact same amount of layers as the Norway race) and jumped on the metro to the starting area, which was at the aquatic centre on an island in the river. It was cold, but seeing fellow runners heading to the race in similar gear made me feel that I had dressed appropriately this time and wasn't about to make a fool of myself as the token Brit dressed in too little (or equally too much).

At the start line, I was pretty nervous, more so than usual. This was because I was unsure of whether to wear the Norwegian purchased spikes on my shoes or not. I thought that if I did, all would be OK (aside from making an annoying noise on the parts of the course that may be snow-free), but then I was also thinking that if so much of the route didn't require spikes, then why wear them at all? The only risk was that perhaps I could get to a bit of the course that was worse than I thought and fall and break my leg, meaning an end to many races in future months. Hmm. Decisions. All the locals around me seemed to be spike-free, so what to do?

I spoke to a pacemaker, and she recommended that I go without, so that's what I did. I thought if it felt too dangerous at any point, then I would just walk. This was not going to be a personal best time anyway. The start line was a short five-hundred-metre run from the aquatic centre (where we were gathered), so I made my way up there about fifteen minutes prior to start time. As I got there, it was clear that after only a few seconds of non-movement in that temperature, you really started to feel the cold. I pulled my hat down as far as it would go over my ears and kept my hands under my armpits to stay warm. A text from my mum via her carer ("Good luck. I love you, my marvellous son.") made me smile before I had to put my phone away quickly to stop that from freezing too. It felt like quite a long time to the gun, but eventually, after a few minutes' delay, we were off.

We were on a snow-free road for a few hundred metres and then on light snow across the bridge to another island. The route was due to take us on one circuit of a larger island and then back over to the island where we started for three loops of the smaller island. We weren't allowed to wear headphones (although I did have the song "Let It Go" from the recent Disney film *Frozen* in my head for the entire run), but my breathing didn't seem to sound too bad and all was going OK. Whenever I run without headphones, I always think I sound much more unfit than I should. After about ten minutes, I noticed that my right thumb was feeling frozen, to the point where it stung a little. This couldn't be good! I carried on running whilst trying to blow hot air onto said thumb through my glove, which felt nice for the short second it lasted, before dropping to negative temperatures again. I worried that if it got worse, I may have to stop to warm up properly; otherwise, I would be running the risk of taking the name of the race a little too literally and developing hypothermia, ending up with a blackened thumb that would eventually fall off, which, let's be honest, is never a good look, eh?

Luckily, though, once I warmed up, the blood was flowing well enough through all required body parts and I was really enjoying the race. It was amazing to run in such beautiful surroundings, and the sun was shining off the snow, which made for a pretty sight. The race was fairly flat and being up with the leaders of the race, I was pleased with my progress. I hadn't trained in that type of environment before, so as long as I finished, I would be happy. Soon we crossed back over the bridge to the other island to begin our three laps. A nice surprise on the first straight was to see Laura arriving to support me. A quick shout over and she turned round to give me a smile and a wave. Supporters you actually know always give me a boost, so I think I sped up a little to continue on the course.

It was all going well until we turned to run down the opposite side of the island. It was a straight line, affording lovely views of the frozen river and city, but it was both into a headwind (bloody cold on the face and lips) and in much thicker snow. This stretch (hereafter to be known as the road to hell) was about 1.5 kilometres long, which was tough enough, but the thought of doing it again another two times was pretty bad. Luckily, after the road to hell, there were about five hundred metres on snow-free tarmac, which allowed me to make up time and energy, and just at the top of the hill was where Laura was standing, so again some free energy to be gained from a wave. The rest of the course was through some lovely woods, and running in the snow soon became the norm. On the third time down the road to hell, though, I could feel the muscles in my thighs and bum starting to ache. I think it was a combination of sliding all over the place and the cold that did it. However, I didn't get any major cramps and carried on through to the end. I crossed the line quite tired and was given a bottle of water that already had ice in it due to natural freezing conditions.

I was very happy to finish in sixth place in a time of one hour, twenty-nine minutes, and twenty-five seconds, which was slightly slower than my Norway run, but it was definitely a harder route (weird that I got the same finishing place, though). Therefore, I was not too far outside the medals (and was second in the thirty to thirty-nine age group), but then again, those locals did have a home advantage over me, right? (Am I a sore loser, perhaps?)

Joking aside, I had a fantastic race and would recommend this event to people, even if it's just for the free brunch and snowflake-shaped medal they give you at the end. It was a lot harder than the Norway race, and this time I did have blood on my sock for some unknown reason.

Socks all washed and another city done – now only nine left. Eek!

Target: 23
Completed: 14

Chapter 17

Moscow – From Russia with Pink Love

Olympic year: 1980
Moscow Olympic fact: Misha the bear was the first time an
Olympic mascot was widely used at a Summer Olympic Games.

In 1980, the year Ronald Regan became president of the United States, Zimbabwe (formerly Rhodesia) gained independence, the Iran-Iraq war began, I was born, and the Summer Olympics took place in Moscow.

This was the first time that any games were due to take place in Eastern Europe with some of the events being held in Minsk and Kiev, which are now no longer part of the Russian Federation but capitals of their own countries (Belarus and Ukraine, respectively). The 1980 games, however, were surrounded by controversy, as sixty-five countries boycotted and did not compete at the Olympics. The boycott was led by the United States due to then–President Jimmy Carter's stance against the Soviet war in Afghanistan. The games still, however went ahead.

When it came time for me to compete in Moscow, I was excited about the prospect. I had been to Moscow before, when I was on an Interrailing holiday around Eastern Europe, and since then I had also been in St. Petersburg for the White Nights Festival in midsummer. I had loved both trips. Russia has a lot of history, some fine architecture, excellent ballet, the circus, and vodka, so I really wanted to go back. However, at the time of planning my trip in late 2013, Russia was getting ready to host the Winter Olympics in Sochi in February 2014. Exciting to do one of my events in a country that was to be an Olympic host in that very same year, I thought. That was until June 2013, when the president of Russia (Vladimir Putin) passed a federal law which banned the promotion of homosexuality to young people under the age of eighteen. This included any kind of public demonstration of gay rights, material on the subject matter, or simply even displaying tendencies of "nontraditional sexual relationships".

Naturally, huge controversy erupted, with many politicians, celebrities, and civilians speaking out that the Olympics should be moved and the International Olympic Committee (IOC) should find an alternate venue, as the safety of athletes and spectators possibly could not be guaranteed. Given that Russia had spent more on the Sochi Games than was spent on all the other Winter Olympics combined, the games were not moved and were still set to take place as planned.

To try to ensure a successful games which focused on the sport rather than anything else, the IOC clarified rule number fifty of the Olympics, which states, "No kind of demonstration or political, religious, or racial propaganda is permitted," meaning that athletes could make a stand against the anti-gay laws but it must be done away from accredited areas and thus not steal focus from the Olympics itself.

So perhaps the games would go ahead without much focus on the new law. However, when I read articles stating that some Russians, like the actor Ivan Okhlobystin, had written to the president asking for homosexuals to be "burnt in ovens" and for the re-criminalization of homosexuality, it added even more fuel to the fire (no pun intended). Anti-gay groups were arranging "dates" with local gay people online and upon meeting them were beating them and filming it to post online later. Truly horrendous.

Social media saw a frenzy of people asking others to boycott not only the Olympics but also products that were manufactured by Russian companies or in Russia. It was a very hot topic (my favourite hashtag of the moment being #HomoPromo), and I completely support the need to stand up against such ridiculous laws, but I questioned whether, as a gay man, I should run in Russia.

An acquaintance posted this on Facebook the week before the Winter Olympics were due to start:

> *It is really unfair to make Russia a laughing stock. Whatever local difficulties are being experienced are more down to those at the top than those proud people who are just trying to make it work and show the world their best side. Local Sochi people have very limited experience with foreigners at all[,] let alone the rabidly sensational Western press. Let's give the locals a break, knuckle down, and try to enjoy some great sporting achievement and competition and* not *be distracted by the other nonsense which (and I repeat) is* not *the preserve of your average Joe Blow here. The Big Wigs have a lot to answer for. Not the ordinary people who just want to do their best with what they've got to make [guests] feel welcome.*

This made me start to feel that I shouldn't be avoiding Russia as the media in the UK would suggest.

The Olympics went ahead in Sochi as planned (and I did watch and love it). After a little further reading after the Olympics, I found the quote below from a journalist who also happened to be gay:

> *In good conscience, I cannot equate the prejudices of a country's leader to the games; if that were the case, I would have called for boycotts of the former Sarajevo, Greece, China, Mexico, Germany, and some would say the United States. The ideals of*

the Olympic Games must rise above politics, and for the most part, I think Sochi did just that. The games, while not without problems, appeared to be well managed and secure; in today's world, that is the most we can ask for. There is no doubt [that] Putin is an ill-advised, narrow-minded bigot who doesn't deserve to be elevated on the world stage, not only because of his views on gays but also because of numerous other atrocities. However, *the people of Russia, and most importantly the athletes of the Sochi Games, shouldn't be punished because of one idiot's views on the world.* –Kendall0428 @Gay50Blog

My sister still said that I should be careful if I went to Russia. After more research, I found an article on Pink News, quoting broadcaster Alice Arnold. Here is what she said:

There have been calls for gay athletes and commentators to boycott the games. This strikes me as bizarre. Surely these are the very people who need to be there. If there was to have been any kind of boycott, it has to come from everyone, not just the gay minority. During apartheid in South Africa, we would not have said to black cricketers, "You stay at home while the white people play." When the boycott came, it came from all players, black and white. Let's remember that it was only ten years ago that Section 28 was repealed in this country [the UK]. Section 28 was very similar to the anti-gay laws that now apply in Russia. A lot can happen in ten years. But it doesn't happen by staying at home and doing nothing. The gay competitors and commentators are no more responsible for trying to change attitudes than everyone else [is]. So let's hope for a real sense of community and support for all diversity from everyone. Watch that, Putin, and enjoy the show.

Well said, I thought, therefore deciding that I wanted to and should go to Russia and compete. So on to Moscow it was. I entered a seven-kilometre race to vary once again the distances I was running. I had never run a race of this distance before, so a PB was guaranteed.

It did seem that Moscow would continue to be the most controversial of all the Olympic cities.

At the end of 2013, Steven and I had gone on a long weekend in Ukraine. We visited Kiev and took a daytrip out to visit Chernobyl which was a surreal but fascinating day. At the time, everything seemed peaceful in Kiev, yet only a few weeks later, extremely violent protests broke out, with many people killed. As time went on, the unrest was focused around the Crimea region of the country and whether it should become part of Russia rather than Ukraine, which was edging towards becoming part of the EU. Russia essentially took control of Crimea by way of what was considered by many states to be an illegal referendum, leaving some people in Crimea unsure of how their lives would be moving forward. The unrest was lengthy and involved many other nations, including the UK and the United States, and it was still not resolved by the time we were due to head to Russia. None of the trouble had taken place in Moscow itself, but it was another area for us to be vigilant of when we were there.

So with boyfriend in tow, I then prepared to set off to Moscow (albeit to stay in a twin room). The first challenge was getting a Russian visa. As I mentioned, I had travelled to Russia a couple of times before, yet the visa application process does not get any easier. Any visa application centre which has to send all applicants over to a set of PCs to amend their online applications because information is missing from the form has an issue somewhere. Why not make the form so that you cannot complete the online form unless all the necessary information is there? Even when I took back Steven's amended form, the woman behind the counter kept asking me if I would pick up my application, when you would have thought that one of the first checks might be to look at the photo on the passport and application and thus see it was in fact not me. Frustrating as these processes are, you learn that the only way to deal with it is to smile and carry on; otherwise, you get nowhere. Despite that, we got a visa and on to the Russian Federation it was.

When we arrived in Moscow, it immediately felt great to be back in such a fantastic city. Walking into Red Square is a feeling that can only be felt and not described. There are so many iconic buildings in one place that it is quite overwhelming, despite having been there before. We spent the first two days of our long weekend seeing the sights (you guessed it: partially by open-top bus) as well as browsing the many stalls offering Russian dolls at a local market, with my favourite being one that was actually painted as Michael Jackson, with each doll becoming progressively blacker. Very inappropriate. I didn't buy a doll because I already had one from the previous trip and because I can't stand Russian dolls because they are full of themselves. Bad joke. Apologies for that one.

The night before the race, it was time to carb up. We had read about an American-style diner (in terms of its decor) that served traditional Soviet food. We were sold and decided this would be the place for me to overload on food. They had an English menu, but we still weren't sure what most of the things on the menu were, so it was a bit of a guessing game. However, all turned out OK. We had some dumplings for starters and pasta and meat for mains. Stuffed, I felt fully fed for the run the next day.

I was able to register for the race at the start line, which was handy because the run was actually taking place in a large park on the outskirts of the city so it wouldn't have been time efficient to spend time going out there when there were others things to be seen in central Moscow.

By the time I arrived at the station stop, I had already spotted what I thought was a fellow runner on the train and opted to follow her. We started talking whilst trying to find the park, which was nice. As in Montreal, I was the only non-local running in the event, so they had quite an interest as to why I was there. The woman told me that it was a small event and had sold out in three days, so she was a little perplexed as to how I even found out about the race to begin with. She said that the organiser was a well-known man and had actually wanted to hold the event in the city centre but the government had not allowed it.

At registration, I picked up my number and timing chip with no hassle and was ready for the race. There were family races beforehand, which were fun to watch, and there were even a few zombies in the registration area (for what purpose I could not figure out). The race was seven kilometres but those feeling more energetic could continue for a farther two laps in order to complete a half marathon.

Ten minutes before the start, they separated us into starting pens and the countdown was off. We set out across the park under glorious sunshine. It was a real treat to be running in such an open space after being in the city for a few days. The park was pretty undulating, and the route took in some sharp 180-degree turns, but I was making good pace as I passed each kilometre marker. I was a little smug going past each mark, as it had the number for those runners that would have to endure a second and a third lap, and I knew I would be done fairly soon.

The run had a subtitle of "Drum & Race", and along the route, there were local drum bands giving us support, which was pretty cool. Nice play on words too. Soon I was in the final kilometre and looking forward to seeing Steven at the end. I had been a little worried about the end because I thought I would need to run left back to the line where we started and others would continue on another loop to the right, but I wasn't 100 per cent sure. As I saw Steven, he shouted that I should indeed turn right, despite the marshal pointing left! I crossed the line and was happy that the fifteenth city in my Olympic challenge was now complete. I finished in fourth place overall (out of the 419 registered for the seven-kilometre race), in a time of twenty-six minutes on the nose. This was a PB, as I had never done a seven-kilometre race (or ever so slightly longer, as each loop needed to make up the distance to a half marathon in the end) – so overall, it was a good run. While walking back to the train station, the compère of the event did a quick interview with me, and I think he was a little surprised that I was not Russian, but it was nice to hear the summary back to the crowd in Russian. I can only hope and assume he translated what I said and didn't alter it into anything unflattering.

After the run, I enjoyed a cocktail on the roof of a hotel overlooking Red Square and the Kremlin, which was awesome. Had the drinks not been quite so ridiculously expensive, I would have happily stayed there all night, but alas, we needed to find a cheaper venue. We located a more standard price range bar. Drinks were drunk, and then I was drunk.

Moscow was a fantastic place to be back in, and I really enjoyed having a shorter run to take part in versus my usual distance. I didn't feel any threat from either of the political stances that I mentioned earlier, and I am pleased that I fully researched the situation and didn't let the media put me off going there.

Target: 23
Completed: 15

Almost done in Beijing

Amsterdam

Barcelona

Beijing Triathlon

Berlin Race

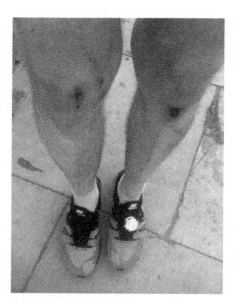

Bloody knees in Barcelona

Cheeky in London

Clourful in London

Day of the Dead in Mexico City

Disney finish

Drag in London

Flag with a difference in Mexico City

helsinki run

Istanbul start

Lunch of champions in Paris

Melbourne race

Montreal race

More drag in London

Munich finish

Pretending to be pro in Moscow

Photo shoot in Rio

Rio finish

Rome Run

Russia Race

Seoul race   St Louis finish

Stay strong and positive. Message from Atlanta

Stockholm Run

Sydney race

Tokyo run

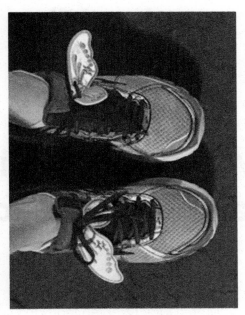

Wings make you run faster

Wrapped up in Montreal

Chapter 18

Sydney – The City Versus the Beach

Olympic year: 2000
Sydney Olympic fact: Over ten thousand athletes
from 199 countries took part in the games,
making it the biggest in history at the time.

Back in 1994, I remember watching TV at my house in Brussels when Sydney was awarded the Olympic Games for the year 2000. I was excited because I'd always held an interest in the city and Australia (having gained most of my knowledge on the country and culture by watching *Neighbours*). When the Olympics took place (and my culture knowledge was a little wider now that I was twenty), I thoroughly enjoyed the show the country put on, especially since the closing ceremony included a performance by Kylie Minogue. I told you my culture barometer had been on the up.

After university, I spent six months travelling and bought a round-the-world ticket. I spent the majority of my trip in Australia and based myself in Sydney for three months. I loved the city from the start. It has a fantastic buzz. It's beautiful and fun. I cannot recommend it enough to anyone, and I genuinely believe you would be struggling to find people who don't enjoy themselves there.

So when it came to heading back there for my Olympic run, I was very excited and booked my flights eleven months in advance, using my air miles. It was going to have been almost twelve years since I had been in the city, so I was uber-ecstatic. The journey down under was long but thankfully uneventful. I was actually travelling on Malaysia Airlines, which sadly had fallen victim to two fatal crashes in the three months before my trip, but despite some concerned faces from friends and colleagues, I didn't have any worries about travelling with them. This clearly was not the case for the nervous man seated next to me, who immediately upon our meeting asked if I had heard about the incidents involving the airline (who in the world hadn't?). Throughout the flight, he kept a firm eye on the moving map, although what he would have done if he saw us veering off course, I do not know. We were travelling on the A380 super jumbo, and whilst that was very exciting for me, as a plane geek, it did seem to concern him somewhat that the engines were so quiet, convincing him that something was wrong and we were descending. At this time, it was clear I should use my headphones to watch a movie and block out his worried tones from my eardrums.

Twenty-four hours later, I was back in Sydney. For a short while, I almost didn't think that they were going to let me into the country as I was taken off for a mini interview at immigration. Yikes. I was once stopped (incorrectly I may add) by a sniffer dog when I got to New Zealand. They took me off saying they would have to conduct an internal body search (at which point I wondered if I could pick the customs officer that conducted said search) but all jokes aside, I was pretty nervous. No searches were undertaken but it still makes me sweat every time I am not allowed through immigration immediately. However; this time after only a few minutes it was clear that this time I was just one of the random checks and before long I would be on my way into the city itself. Once I reached town it really felt like my old stomping ground and within the first few hours, I had been around the harbour, visited where I used to live and had made my way to the race expo to pick up my race number for the race which was taking place three days later.

The race I had entered was called the City2Surf. It is a fourteen-kilometre run that starts in Hyde Park, in the heart of Sydney, and takes runners to a well-deserved finish on the world famous Bondi Beach. Upon getting my number, I realised that I was in the fourth start wave. I have to admit that I was a little miffed about starting that far back, for I knew the crowds would be big and therefore it may affect my performance when and if I needed to dodge around people. I had been told that there had been eighty-two thousand people entered into the race, and whilst I could not claim that I was elite, I did think that I could at least keep up with the first wave. I asked if it was possible to move up a group but was told that it wasn't; moreover, if anyone tried to enter the incorrect "pen" on the day, the person would be disqualified. Harsh, but I understood. Organising such an event does take some preparation, and people trying to change things last minute would not help. So with that in mind, I realised I would just have to enjoy the day and take in the atmosphere of the event. It was sure to be a good one with that many people involved, so I was still looking forward to the run.

Looking around the rest of the expo, I came across a guy (Chris) selling a book which he had written about the City2Surf. The inaugural race was held in 1971, which he had taken part in, as well as every single one thereafter. His book covered the history of the race and also included interviews with the other "legends", those who had also completed every race since it began. While he and I were chatting, we shared running stories and he gave me a few tips about the race, which were much appreciated. I told him about my Olympic challenge, which he was interested in, and he kindly signed a copy of his book for me. I had already been told about "Heartbreak Hill", which many found to be the impossible part of the City2Surf. I asked Chris about it, and he told me that as a runner who had done a fair bit of hill training, I would not find it too difficult. He said that the reason the hill had been christened a heartbreaker was not due to the severity of the ascent but merely because it was such a long stretch of two kilometres that it often seemed it was coming to an end, but around each corner lay slightly more hill. That made me feel good and that perhaps it was going to be a rather fast course for me. Regardless, it was guaranteed to be a PB because I had never completed a fourteen-kilometre race, so no matter what happened on the day, I could be sure of something to celebrate. Even more excited for the race now, I returned to my hotel for an early night, as it had been a long journey.

In the days leading up to the race, I continued to see parts of the city I used to enjoy, like Manly Beach and the botanical gardens. I had also arranged to meet up with a school friend I hadn't seen for sixteen years. We met in a rooftop bar overlooking the harbour, intending to catch up over a glass of champagne or two at most. Before I knew it, our planned couple of drinks turned into a mammoth champagne fest and I was shit-faced. It was so much fun but very different from my usual race preparation of no drinking and healthy food. I suppose I could say that I didn't eat unhealthily, as I didn't eat at all that night (we all know eating is cheating, right?). Oh well ... If I was due to start quite far back in group four of the race, then a little bit of overindulgence wouldn't hurt. Plus, I had two days to recover anyway.

The next day, I was luckily hangover-free and went out shopping for the day. I went to some markets and squeezed in a morning tour on a Harley Davidson that took me across the Harbour Bridge, which was awesome and blew away the cobwebs from said champagne fest. I then went up the Sydney Tower to do the SKYWALK on the glass bottom floor, which actually required me to have a breath test to ensure I was not intoxicated. I passed, which must have meant that I hadn't had too much champagne the night before and maybe we should have stayed for one more.

The night before race day, I was much better behaved and carbed up, making sure I only drank bubbles that came in the format of sparkling water. I was in bed early and got a good night's sleep, despite a slight misshape of a midnight toilet break that led me to walk into the corner of the wardrobe and cut my head open. Oops.

It stopped bleeding after a while, which meant I would be OK for race day, but I would look a little odd with a cut down my forehead. Maybe given that I also have a heavy English accent, people would mistake me for an old Harry Potter with his lightening scar? Maybe? No? OK, then let's move on.

On race day, it was an early start, and despite it being winter in the Southern Hemisphere, it wasn't too cold, especially for my English skin. Chatting to a few locals in the pens before kick-off, they did think I was a little crazy only being in a vest whilst they waited patiently for the start gun in their jackets with cups of coffee. I told them that I was from the UK and this seemed positively tropical compared to the wait for race starts in the UK in March. They laughed, and I then felt even warmer.

The race was well organised, and whilst I was in the fourth start group, each wave was actually leaving twenty minutes apart, which meant that provided I was at the head of my group when the gun went off, I would get a good start and it wouldn't be as crowded as I had thought. The atmosphere was excellent and building to a palpable level. DJ Red Foo was kicking out the tunes, and the Commonwealth Marathon winner from a few weeks prior in Glasgow, Michael Shelley, was due to set us off with the start gun. All this being under the setting of the city was getting the butterflies in my tummy moving. Soon enough, the elites went off, followed closely by the top charity fundraisers and then by another group before it was the blue group's turn (which included me).

We made our way away from the park and down a hill, which sadly was short-lived and suddenly turned into an uphill climb. I had been warned that Heartbreak Hill was slap bang in the middle of the race between the sixth and seventh kilometres, but nobody had told me about this first one. WTF! If this one didn't merit a mention, what was Heartbreak Hill going to be like? I started to doubt what Chris had told me a mere forty-eight hours previously and wondered if he was just trying to make me feel better at the expo.

Negative thoughts aside, I made it over the first hill and we carried on through the city and past some of the lovely bays that were filled with numerous yachts, which was a fantastic view. The course was overall a lot more undulating than I had anticipated, but as we neared the halfway point, we got a look back over the harbour towards the Harbour Bridge and the Opera House – amazing and definitely an energy boost to the system. So being half way through it meant only one thing: Heartbreak Hill was here. It hurt. A lot. I can concur that Chris was right that it was not that steep all the way through; however, the start was most definitely a hill and the corners seemed to keep coming.

At this point in the race, I had caught up with the group that had set off before me and a lot of them were choosing to walk up this almost mountain. I managed to keep running throughout, but I definitely slowed down to what felt like the most uncoordinated running style. My coach always says that when going uphill or when you are feeling tired to really use your arms, for it will naturally make your legs keep going. I used my arms a lot and made it to the top. Once we passed the eight-kilometre mark, I knew the hard part was over and we were into the second part of the course and on the home straight (albeit quite a long home straight). As I mentioned, I had at this point caught up with the previous group and had to run on the pavement to ensure I didn't get in the way of other runners to overtake, but I was thoroughly enjoying the race.

The sidelines were packed with supporters, and we soon passed the ten-kilometre mark. I can honestly say the last four kilometres really flew by (maybe because large portions were downhill?). It wasn't the fastest four kilometres I have ever run, but it did feel like it. Not really quite sure why, though.

Bondi Beach was soon in sight. We came down the hill to the beach, and over the finish line I went. My result:

Overall time: fifty-five minutes and fifty-one seconds
Place: 646th out of 67,527 finishers

My average speed for each kilometre before the hill was three minutes and forty-two seconds versus four minutes and twenty-three seconds during the hill and four minutes and ten seconds post-hill. Clearly, Heartbreak Hill took its toll.

The finish at the beach was fantastic, especially seeing runners cool their feet off in the waves amongst surfers. I waited at the finish line for a couple of school friends who were running the race too, and it was great to see them at the finish line after two years of being apart. Sadly, as I was waiting, I saw a young man being stretchered off from the finish line and thought he was unconscious. The next morning it was announced that a man of twenty-seven had died at the finish of the race after suffering cardiac arrest. I can't be sure it was the gentleman that I saw, but from the images I witnessed on the news, I am pretty sure it was. It is ever so sad when something like that happens, and you can only hope that he didn't suffer too much.

After the race, I met some family for a rather boozy afternoon lunch in central Sydney, which was great fun, followed by a couple of days of more sightseeing in the form of a wine tasting trip to the Hunter Valley (alcohol theme for the trip emerging?) and climbing the Sydney Harbour Bridge. I love the city and the City2Surf and hope to be back someday to run it again (despite the nine minutes of heartbreak in the middle).

So that took me to sixteen cities completed, and in a mere seven days, it was to be the turn of fellow Australian city Melbourne.

Target: 23
Completed: 16

Chapter 19

Melbourne – The Best City on Earth

Olympic year: 1956
Melbourne Olympic fact: It's the only time the games
have been shared between two countries. Equestrian
events took place in Stockholm due to the Australian
government not allowing foreign horses into the country.

So after a fantastic time in Sydney, it was time to head to Melbourne. I had been to the city once before (again, during my backpacker days), but only for a week, so I didn't know it well.

I now had numerous friends from school and university living in the city so I had planned lots of reunions as well as the run whilst I was in town. I was happy to be there. Upon arriving (via low-cost airline Tigerair), I touched down at the shed they call Terminal 4. It can't be classed as the best terminal ever, but it got me to my next Olympic city, so I can't complain. On the short bus ride into town, I recognised parts of the city, but it certainly felt much larger than twelve years before and had a lot more skyscrapers than I remembered. The week I arrived, Melbourne had been voted the best place in the world to live for the fourth year running. That plus the fact that I was staying with friends the entire week meant I would get to experience the best of the city from a local's point of view; I was excited.

The race I had entered was a half marathon and was being organised by a local running club called the Victorian Road Runners. I had found the race on their site, working out perfectly that I could find two races so close together, given that it would have been a bit of an effort to come Down Under for one race and then make the trip again another time for the second one. I was a little dubious that the race would go ahead, for the club's website said that runners just needed to turn up on the day and pay twenty dollars to run. It was very different from the massive event the week before, but I was looking forward to it.

In the days leading up to the race, I met friends, drank, ate, shopped in the trendy Fitzroy area of town, visited an art fair, swam in the outdoor (heated) city pool, and watched two of my friends (who were planning to run the half marathon with me) suffer some of the worst hangovers I have ever seen. Who knew it could take forty minutes to eat a piece of toast! I also found out that whilst coffee is a big part of Australian culture, it seemed even more so in Melbourne. I have never drunk so much of the stuff, and whilst it was enjoyable, I think my heart was certainly beating much quicker than usual!

Melbourne was certainly a fun place to be to catch up with friends, and it is a very different vibe to that of Sydney. The fun and sights in Melbourne are much less obvious than in Sydney. There is no equivalent of Sydney Harbour, but the fashion, bars, and restaurants seemed much more on-trend than those in Sydney. After a few decadent days, it was soon the night before the race, and my friends and I decided on a night in to carb up and try to rid them both of the aforementioned hangovers.

The race was due to start at 8 a.m. on the Sunday and was only a two-kilometre walk from their house, so it wasn't a ridiculously early start for us. It was a little earlier for me because I like to have a big bowl of porridge and three bananas (much to the horror of friends, who can't believe I can eat that many bananas in one go) before doing a big race, so I needed a bit of time to digest all of that. The race was in Princes Park, in the north of the city. Arriving at the park, there were probably about one hundred people, and we all paid our entrance fee for the race. We all received handwritten numbers to place on our shirts.

The main race organiser then gathered us round to brief us on the course. I immediately thought that since I was not familiar with the area, I would simply follow the person in front, until said organiser began his speech by saying that people seemed to immediately turn dumb as soon as they put on a pair of trainers and will follow the person in front, meaning that if the leader went wrong, then so did the entire group. OK, so that made me one of the dumb ones, then. He explained that the course would be made up of one full lap of the park, followed by four larger laps that took in part of the park and Melbourne Cemetery, which was adjacent to the park itself. It sounded simple enough, but I have to admit that I was not particularly looking forward to doing five laps. As you may remember from my Moscow race (where I opted to do the shorter race in order to avoid further laps of the same course), here I had no option but to man up and get ready in my head for lap running.

Setting off, the leaders were going at a similar pace to mine, which was good and made the first lap enjoyable. There were three of us running together up to this point, but the third person started to drop behind. This left two of us running side by side for the first of the larger laps. Whilst this may sound very social, the only words passed between us was when he asked me what time I was aiming for. He was clearly aiming for a quicker time because soon after this, he sped up and left me about one hundred metres behind. I was actually quite pleased that he did because I felt quite a weird sense of pressure to keep up when we were side by side; at least this way, I would get to run at a pace that I liked. Sounds not very competitive of me to give up that easily, but my goal was to finish in the top three, so I was still on track for achieving that.

The laps went fairly quickly, and at the end of each one, I would tick off in my head the percentage of the race that I had completed.

This made it much easier to get through another lap of the same thing. The course (I avoided saying *route* there, as it means something completely different and a little rude in Australia) was fairly flat. The park was pretty quiet and picturesque, and the outskirts of the cemetery that I saw looked impressive. Along one side of the park, we ran next to the cemetery, which had a high fence. The rising sun felt lovely on the skin, but when running down a hill, it created a strobe light effect which left me feeling a little dizzy after the first time, let alone the following three times. The hill became known in my head as "Strobe Light Hill" thereafter. To rival Sydney's hill offering from the week before, there was also a slight incline on the other side of the cemetery to strobe light hill, which became known to me as "Horrendous Hill". It wasn't a steep incline or even particularly lengthy, but it did hurt, and the fact that it came around every eighteen minutes throughout the race played havoc with my mood.

Soon enough, though, the last lap was upon me. The leader was still about one hundred metres or so ahead of me, and I knew that unless something drastic happened, I would finish in second place. The last kilometre took an age to complete, but the finish line eventually was behind me. I finished in a time of one hour, twenty-one minutes, and forty-one seconds. It was not a personal best but still a pretty solid time, and I was happy to be taking home a medal of the silver variety. The event was only giving out medals for the first three winners, so getting a souvenir was a total bonus. My running coach had won silver at the Commonwealth Games when it was in Melbourne in 2006, so it meant I could text her and say that I was now in the same spectrum and had silverware from Melbourne too (albeit not quite from the same level of athletics as hers, but still). I cheered the other runners over the line – in particular, my two friends who had by this point definitely run out their hangovers from the night before and completely smashed their PBs.

The organisers did a little ceremony for the medals, which turned out to be quite funny. I was called up for my second place, and shortly after that, they called my friend Mark's name to come and collect his medal for third place. I was confused, and Mark looked even more so. Silence followed, and then Mark put his hand up to say that they had indeed called his name but he definitely didn't come in third. We all laughed, and they corrected the results to call out the correct name of the Mark name who had finished in third place.

Post-race we enjoyed a nice hot shower (not all together, I might add) and some hearty food. We spent the afternoon at an Aussie rules football match at the MCG, which was fantastic. It was a brilliant venue and atmosphere, and to top it off, they let us onto the pitch after the match to throw a few balls about. I was told that it was a rarity to be allowed onto the pitch, so it was a real treat. It could only have been made better with an appearance of my dear Minogue ladies (Dannii and Kylie), who hail from Melbourne. It really was quite selfish of them not to pop by and say hello given that for the entire trip, all I had listened to on my iPod was my "Minogue Magic" playlist.

So my Australian adventure was ending, but not before I made my way back to Sydney for another week. I was lucky enough that work had an office there so I could work for a few days and put off the long journey home for a little longer.

I loved Melbourne (or Melbs, as I started to call it), and it meant the final Olympic run for 2014 was over. I would now have seven months to wait until the next one in Seoul; however, I would have plenty more races back in the UK to keep me busy and perhaps allow me to break the current PB I had.

Target: 23
Completed: 17

Chapter 20

Seoul – Back to the Marathon

Olympic year: 1988
Seoul Olympic fact: Greg Louganis retained his
Olympic diving titles despite cutting his head open
on the diving board during a practice session.

It had been seven months since my last Olympic run. I had had many races in the UK, but it felt good to get back to my challenge. I had my eye on the Seoul International Marathon as my event to do in Seoul but wasn't sure whether I would have the inclination to do another full marathon. It had been just over three years since my last one.

I kept an eye on the website for confirmation of when the race would take place. The organisers had told me that it was usually held in March but they wouldn't finalise the date until a few months before. I wasn't sure I would have enough time to train once they had sorted the date, so I simply left it up to fate to decide whether this would be the event for me or not. I checked back on the website every few weeks to see if anything had changed. Months went by, and it still just had the information from 2014's race. Then one day early in the New Year, the site refreshed and there it was. It was due to be on 15 March 2015. Therefore, I would have three months to train. Was it possible? I knew I would be able to get around the course; the question was how quickly could I do it? I secretly had wanted to be able to call myself a sub-three-hour marathon runner, but I wasn't sure I could achieve this in the time I had to train.

I decided to go with my instinct and enter. As I went through the sign-up pages, I noticed that there was a ten-kilometre race on the same day. I thought that this would be the easy option and almost ticked the box. Something held me back, and I went for the marathon instead. No going back. I told my coach that I had a marathon in three months' time. She laughed and said, "We need to change your training plan, then." We had to make sure that I covered enough miles each week in training in order to be race ready.

My training consisted of five runs per week, the long one being on a Sunday, with the distance quickly increasing to fourteen, sixteen, eighteen, and twenty miles. It took me back to when I was training for both the previous two marathons in Athens and Orlando. My long training route would typically have me heading from my house in West London out to Heathrow Airport and back. It's not the most glamorous route along the A4, but it's a straight road with few roads to cross over, which meant I could keep going for long periods without a break. I enjoyed the training but must say that my final big training run of twenty-two miles hurt. I took a wrong turn on the way back, which added about half a mile on to what I had planned, sending my mood spiralling down the toilet. I was disappointed that I hadn't managed to maintain my planned marathon pace for the last three miles, which had me thinking that a three-hour result was not going to be at all possible. I was now aiming for a three-hour, fifteen-minute result.

However, my coach reminded me that running on your own is different to the actual event, as there is no support or fellow runners to boost your mood, nor are there planned water and food stations for you to refuel. Good points. With that reasoning, it's clear why she's the coach. So perhaps I would be able to make sub three hours, then. We would have to wait and see.

Training had been going well, and I was hopeful for a good result. I emailed the race organisers and asked them how they determined what start zone I would be in, as I hadn't had to put in my predicted finish time when applying for the race. They informed me that they would only do that by previous marathon results. I told them that my last one was three hours and fifty minutes but I was much fitter now and wanted to aim for three hours or less. They told me that they wouldn't put me in a zone based on what I thought I could do, and on top of that, my previous result was from a race in January 2012 and they would only accept results from December 2012 onwards. They placed me in start zone D (out of zones A–E) and said that it would not be changed. Harsh. I was annoyed for a while but thought back to when this happened in Sydney and then accepted that I would just enjoy the day. I planned to be at the front of zone D, and maybe my performance wouldn't be too affected. It may also mean that it would stop me from going off too fast, so there were some positive aspects to zone the D cloud.

The Seoul Olympics was the first one that I remember taking place. I was eight at the time and remember watching the sprinting. The two main things I recall were Florence Griffith-Joyner and her nails/lycra as well as the Ben Johnson one-hundred-metre drugs scandal. I admired Flo Jo for her style and thought that perhaps I could copy her for this race. Perhaps not. I am not sure I could pull off such a flamboyant look, plus it was due to be very chilly on the day of the marathon, so it would be best to cover up.

Arriving in Seoul was very exciting. It was a much larger city than I imagined and had the hectic atmosphere and smells of other big Asian cities I had been to, such as Hong Kong and Bangkok. The hotel I would call home for the next week was contemporary, centrally located, and had the cutest name ever: Small House Big Door. I spent the first few days exploring the city. First stop was Gangnam. We all have committed the crime of "horse dancing" to "Gangnam Style" at the office party (or perhaps at home), so a visit to this trendy district was a must. There actually was a stage on the main shopping street with the sign above it saying "Gangnam Style", and it played the song when you stepped on it. A tourist's dream and a local's nightmare, I am sure.

That done, I also made a trip down to the Olympic park. It was the biggest Olympic park I have been to. I could imagine what the atmosphere must have been like back in 1988, when it was swarming with spectators and the media. It must have been awesome. Today, though, it was pretty quiet and allowed me to take photos of the peace gate and surrounding area relatively free of other people. There is also an Olympic museum on site, which Steven and I got to enjoy to ourselves – a real treat. It was an interesting museum set over two floors and included the history of the Olympics. It wasn't just focused on the Korean ones. It was a sure-fire way to get me excited for the marathon in seventy-two hours' time.

I then also took the time to head north from Seoul to the DMZ (Demilitarized Zone) and the JSA (Joint Security Area) that lies between South Korea and North Korea. It was an educational trip, where I learnt about the Korean War and what that had left. The DMZ was an area two kilometres on either side of the border between the two countries, which is managed by the United Nations with the sole aim of keeping a ceasefire. Going past the DMZ, we went into the JSA, which was the area directly at the border. We visited offices where officials meet to discuss the political situation (with the border actually running through the middle of the room), so when we walked to the northern end of the room, we were technically in North Korea for a few minutes. It was an interesting day and made me wish that one day the two countries could unify peacefully.

Back in Seoul, I was taking in the sights and foods. I made a visit to a street market one evening for some sustenance. It was thoroughly enjoyable although my stay at my chosen stall was cut short a little by two drunk Korean guys who were ecstatic to talk to someone British. I am all up for mixing with the locals, but when the same questions are coming at you every few minutes, you are sober, and they then want you to talk to their daughter on the phone so she can hear an English voice, the thought of moving on for a post-meal walk was appealing. It did make me laugh that one of them introduced himself and then said to me, "I like pills and British men." Quite an intro, eh? What I think he meant to say was that he liked films and British men. At least that's what I gathered once he then moved on to a discussion of Colin Firth films.

That aside, what was genuinely a little more troublesome than I had banked on was the weather. The first full day in Seoul was absolutely freezing. Literally. It was so cold that walking for eight to ten minutes outside left me looking for the nearest coffee shop in which to get warm. I checked the temperature on my phone. It was minus one degree centigrade. WTF? I hadn't thought it would be this cold. This wasn't meant to be another hypothermic race like in Montreal. I was panicked for a while until I saw that as the week went by, it was due to heat up to a tropical eleven degrees on race day. I calmed down a bit and didn't need to go emergency thermals shopping.

Two days before the race, I picked up my race packet at the race headquarters. In the pack, I read that the Seoul Marathon is the second oldest in the world, after Boston, and this year was celebrating its eighty-sixth year. Who knew it had been going that long? The day before the race, I relaxed at the hotel and carbed myself up, ready for the long haul that beckoned the next day.

Race day was here. I was excited but also quite nervous. The thought of running 26.2 miles was a little daunting, plus I was putting myself under my own pressure of a good time. Nonetheless, I showered, dressed, and ate a glamourous breakfast of Oats So Simple and bananas in my room before heading to the start line in the centre of town.

I got there about fifty minutes before kick-off. What amazed me were the street sellers who had running tops, gloves, and snacks for runners to buy. Selling snacks I get, but who turns up to a race without actually having a T-shirt already on? Someone must, I guess, or it wouldn't be worthwhile for the traders. The atmosphere at the start was good. Everyone was in a cheerful mood, and the warm-up was done to very upbeat K-Pop (which I became a huge fan of during the trip), with some energetic girls leading on a podium in hot pants. I noted a few of the moves for my next night of clubbing.

Lining up at the start, I noticed that the zones themselves were not that big and there actually wasn't a barrier between them. I got into position at the top of zone D, realizing that those around me were aiming at a very different pace. The official pacemakers had balloons with their times on them, and the ones next to me were four hours, ten minutes as well as four hours, twenty minutes. In the race pack, it had said that the cut-off time for completion of the race was five hours, which is a lot shorter than other marathons I have done, but it was clear to me that I was essentially starting at the back of the pack. I thought I could have pushed my way into a zone further ahead but didn't want to cause any issues so I stuck where I was.

As the gun went off, I heard the elites go as well as zones A and B. The rest of us were then held back for an additional five to ten minutes. Then we were off. I crossed the line and felt almost as if we were walking. I am not being disrespectful to those choosing to run at that pace, but for me it was disappointing, as I was worried that being in a crowd of twenty thousand people would make it impossible to get a decent time. However, a few metres in, I noticed I could run on the outside of the crowds and quickly bypass most of the zone ahead. Seeing the first one-kilometre mark I was within my planned kilometre timing and was actually pretty much running alone in the street. It felt weird. By the next kilometre, though, I had caught up with the back of zone B. I was able to weave my way in an out of those I wanted to pass, and when we reached a narrower part of the route, I could run on the pavement to avoid getting in other people's way. Very similar to what had happened in Sydney.

The kilometres seemed to be flying by, and before I knew it, I had passed Steven at the six-kilometre and then sixteen-kilometre markers. It always feels nice to have a boost from your own support. At this point, I passed a competitor who was skipping (as in with a skipping rope). Was he crazy? I cannot imagine doing that for forty kilometres, but he was keeping up a good pace. I hoped he finished OK.

We were running through the area of town where I had been staying and where I had done my last few easy training runs once I arrived in Seoul. There is a sunken river that used to be a motorway, which is stunning. We ran all the way along it and even took in some of the end sections, where the motorway is still there in semi-derelict form. This was urban running at its best. We looped back on ourselves during this section, and this is when I caught a glimpse of the three-hour pacemaker. He was way ahead of me on the other side of the river, so there was no way I was going to catch him, but I thought I seemed to be running at around the same pace. The drinks stations were every five kilometres, and I made sure I filled up on water and iso drinks at each opportunity. I felt good reaching the twenty-kilometre mark and was still tracking good time. I had filled my pockets with jelly beans and at this point started to take a few to keep my sugar levels up. They tasted good.

The route had remained fairly flat, and the kilometres were still going by quickly. At the halfway point, I crossed in about one hour and twenty-two minutes which I knew was fast. I was happy to be on track for sub three hours, and I knew that I had an "extra" eight minutes to do the second half; however, when you break that down, it's not actually that much extra per kilometre.

Just beyond this point, I did have to start planning a recreation of one of Paula Radcliff's most famous moments. Where could I pee? I hadn't really noticed any loos along the route, so searching out for a roadside bush was a must. I had noticed a few people doing this way back at the start, so I figured I would not get arrested for doing the same. I spotted a place with no spectators nearby and made my way off for some relief. I clearly started a trend, as someone then joined me at the same bush. Nice to create a sense of community. Onwards I then went.

As I reached the thirty-kilometre mark, I was still pacing well, but my legs had started to feel a little heavy. There was a food station at this point, so I refuelled with a banana (my fourth of the day so far) and more jelly beans. They were handing out chocolate biscuits at this station too, and I was so tempted to break my no chocolate for lent rule and take one, but I resisted. I'd like to think, though, that you would have forgiven me this one had I succumbed.

I then didn't focus on the rest of the race but merely on getting to the thirty-five kilometre mark, when I would treat myself to more sugar. The kilometres were certainly not flying by from this point, and I could tell I was slowing down. Reaching the thirty-five-kilometre mark, I was happy (particularly as it had been the steepest incline of the race to reach it) and the views across the river were lovely. That said, though, I could see the Olympic stadium where we were due to finish across the other side of the river and realised it was an additional seven kilometres before we would be inside it. That's a long way given how I was feeling at this point. The ten-kilometre race which I had almost entered also joined us at this point, so being passed by upbeat runners who were in their first kilometre had me thinking evil thoughts about them. I parked those thoughts and started to work on a game plan of how I was going to make it to the end. I knew I wouldn't make it within three hours at this stage since my pace had slowed quite a lot. So I focused on beating the three hours and fifteen minutes that I had thought about after my last training run in London. I decided to run each kilometre and then walk for fifteen seconds to rest and then run to the next kilometre marker. This seemed to work for me, and whilst I was disappointed to have to stop for short breaks, I thought it was best to arrive at the finish in one piece.

Soon I was at forty kilometres with only two more to go. I carried on with the same strategy and then there was only one kilometre to go. *Woo-hoo!* I passed Steven again, which made me feel good when he shouted my name, and then I was inside the stadium. Less than once around the track and I would be home. I looked at my watch as I crossed the line: three hours, three minutes, and thirty-six seconds. Almost all threes! It placed me 537th out of 20,000 starters. Maybe next time the organisers would put me in a higher up starting zone. I was super pleased with the result and couldn't quite believe that I had done another full marathon and in such a quick time. That made it one hour and eleven minutes quicker than my first one in Athens.

When I started running five years earlier, I never would have thought that would be possible.

Post-race my legs were a little sore, but I refuelled with yet another banana, making my total five for the day. Perhaps Chiquita are looking for a face to front their campaigns. I am willing to work for smaller charges than most. I also had a can of Coke, more iso drinks, water, and biscuits. All of this recharged my battery, and I was ready for some photos in front of the stadium before a shower back at the hotel. Fellow runners may have experienced the pain of putting on deodorant after a long race, but one new pain I had not experienced before was the shockwave when the hot water hit my balls. My leggings must have been rubbing (unbeknownst to me) throughout the race and created a little red patch on the left one. Ouch.

I thoroughly enjoyed the race, and despite it being tough for the last seven kilometres, I would run a full marathon again. Maybe this time if I could start with the three-hour pacemaker, I would be able to keep with them and break the three-hour mark. Maybe next time. For now, though, I was very pleased with my result. I had now completed my eighteenth Olympic city.

Target: 23
Completed: 18

Chapter 21

Los Angeles – A Run in the Happiest Place on Earth

Olympic Year: 1932 and 1984
Los Angeles Olympic fact: 1984 was the first time that the
women's marathon event was included in the Olympics.

All things Disney are a guilty pleasure of mine. As mentioned back in the Tokyo chapter, I have visited all of the Disney parks worldwide (a true statement until Shanghai opened one in 2016 meaning I now need to go back to China), so when it came to choosing an event to do in Los Angeles, the choice was clear. Girly as it may be, the Tinkerbell Half Marathon in Disneyland was it.

Back at the start of 2012, I had entered Goofy's Race and a Half Challenge in Walt Disney World in Florida, which formed part of the Run Disney race weekend at the park. The challenge was to run the Donald Duck half marathon on Saturday, followed by the Mickey Mouse marathon on Sunday, making up a total of 39.3 miles to be covered in a twenty-four-hour period. Those completing the challenge not only got a medal from each race but the coveted Goofy medal, which also allowed you entry to any of the Disney Parks free of charge the following Monday (provided you could still get out of bed and walk there). My training for this event was fairly hard, and it was difficult to know if I had done enough, as there was no way I could replicate that amount of mileage during a normal weekend of training. However, feeling fit, off I set for Orlando.

I told myself that upon arrival in Disney, I would take it easy and not spend all day and night in the parks (i.e., on my feet), but the fun and atmosphere of the parks was too much for me to resist. The day before the half marathon, I spent a fantastic day at the Magic Kingdom, reliving my youth from when I was last in the park when I was nine. I was fairly sensible, though, and had an early night since the alarm was set for 3 a.m. because the race was due to kick off at 5.30 a.m.

Heading to the start line at Epcot Center, it was fun to see characters along the way, and it took my mind off the cold. An error I made, though, was that when signing up, I had no idea how tired I would feel and how long it would take me to complete both events, so I opted for one of the longest times in the drop-down menu. Gathered in my starting corral, I realized this mistake when I heard people saying that they were aiming for a half marathon time of under four hours. Hmm. Not to sound arrogant, but I knew that I was in the wrong group. Nonetheless I set off and enjoyed the race around Epcot Center and Magic Kingdom. I had to zigzag in and out of people in front of me to get ahead for the first seven miles, but I still was enjoying it and came home in a time of one hour and thirty-six minutes. On a Disney high, I went back to my hotel, showered, and went straight back to Epcot to enjoy an afternoon in the park.

That evening, I texted my Dad back in England to ask him to go online and check that my timing chip had been working, as I was due to use the same one the next day for the marathon. He said he could see my results online and at the same time had noticed that you were able to do online tracking of athletes. He intended to do that for the marathon in a few hours' time. I had an early night in the hotel, having a bath and ordering a pizza to carb up. I thought ordering one pizza and garlic bread should have been sufficient, but when my order arrived at my room in four separate boxes, I remembered that US portion size somewhat differs from European ones; I had enough to feed a family of four.

Stuffed to capacity, I managed a few hours' sleep before 3 a.m. rolled round again for the 5.30 a.m. race start. Upon arrival at the start area, I was upgraded to the first corral based on my performance from the day before, which meant that I would spend less time passing others and thus save on energy for the long run to the finish line. The run this time took us through all four of the Disney parks: Magic Kingdom, Epcot, Hollywood Studios, and Animal Kingdom. It was a great run, and the change in scenery and the Disney characters on the sidelines kept everyone's spirits up and faces smiling.

I was on this trip alone, so as I approached the twenty-mile mark, I started to think that I would like some of my own support and was going to ring my parents and have a little comfort stop at twenty-two miles. As I went past the twenty-one-mile marker, though, a text came through on my phone. As I looked down, I saw it was from my Dad, saying that he had seen I was past the twenty-mile mark and doing really well and to keep going. Filled with excitement by this message, I no longer needed the pit stop at twenty-two miles and carried on through, knowing the end was (almost) in sight.

Along the way, characters from Mickey and Minnie to Chip and Dale had lined the streets, and all runners could stop to have a photo with them. The queue to do this had been pretty long, but now that I was almost at the end, I didn't have many runners around me. Because I was in the leading pack, there was no wait to stop for a photo op with a character. I had read a book called *Cast Member Confidential* prior to my trip, which documented the true experience of an employee at Disney in Orlando. He had described how the employees (known as cast members) playing the role of characters were never allowed to break character at any point whilst interacting with the public. A tough job, I thought, but a fact I had forgotten in my thirty-eight miles of running in one day. So as I was in the last mile of the race, I decided to stop for a picture with Aladdin. As I stood next to him, he asked what everyone was running for. Confused, I asked him to repeat the question and again he enquired what everyone was running from. "How should we escape? Where should we go?" *WTF?* I thought. *What is he talking about?* Then it dawned on me that in the film, Aladdin was always on the run, so he was just in character. After our photo together, he sent me on my way, wishing me luck and saying that he and Aboo (his monkey) would catch up with us once they managed to escape. A bizarre but hilarious experience.

After crossing the line in a time of three hours and fifty minutes, it was fantastic to have completed the challenge and get the Goofy medal. Post-race I spent a few days on the beach drinking cocktails in Miami and returned to England thoroughly having enjoyed the trip. With this in mind, you can see why I was excited at the prospect of another run in Disney – this time in the original Disney park in Los Angeles.

I was too young to appreciate the Los Angeles Olympics when they happened, but as I got more into long-distance running, I learnt that the 1984 Olympics was the first time that a marathon race had taken place for women and the winner was a woman called Joan Benoit. I was lucky enough to meet her during a trip to Bermuda, and it felt great to meet my first Olympic Gold medallist. I told her about my Olympic challenge, but as she had a queue of people waiting to see her, she either didn't hear me properly or didn't find it too interesting, for she didn't seem too fussed over it. Oh well, it still was great to meet her.

So on to LA it was. I love the city and had my friends Laura, Claire, and Sophie in tow. We were going to be in Los Angeles for a week. First celebrity spot/meet of the holiday was Niall from One Direction, who was on our flight. He posed nicely for a selfie, despite our having One Direction Top Trumps in our possession. So with Sophie still shaking from shock at meeting one of her idols, we made our way to West Hollywood, where we would be spending our first few days.

During the following days, we spent time on Hollywood Boulevard (in the non-prostitute sense), had drinks at the Rainbow Bar and Grill, ate ridiculous-sized portions of food, enjoyed a cocktail at No Vacancy (Google how you enter that bar – or better still, go find out for yourself), had a manicure, hiked in the Hollywood hills, and went shopping at Jimmy Choo on Rodeo Drive. If I ever win the lottery, I intend to buy Jimmy Choo. Not just a new pair of shoes – the actual man so that I can have shoes on tap forever. So with new shoes purchased, it was time for our last night in West Hollywood.

We had spotted a burger joint called Hamburger Mary's, which we thought looked good. We went in and got a table. The only one left was in front of a little stage. Quickly it was apparent that the establishment was also a drag bar. We enjoyed strong cocktails, good burgers, and the hilarious show that followed. Of course, being the front table, we had a good view and were prime victims for the drag queens performing. I didn't escape unscathed and involuntarily became part of the show for a few minutes. Post-show we carried on for a few more drinks and shots and retired to bed/passed out at 3 a.m. The next day we enjoyed a spot-on brunch on Sunset Boulevard, including a health shot to clear the system. We were so LA.

We then made our way out to Anaheim for Disneyland. On arrival at our hotel, I made a quick dash through Downtown Disney to register for the event. It cannot be denied that the Run Disney events are organized with complete precision. They may be among the most expensive races I have entered, but they are worth every penny. Number collected and fairy wings for my trainers purchased, I was ready for the race the next day. Disney had kindly arranged for the premier of the film *Tomorrowland* to be taking place that evening, so we caught an up-close glimpse of George Clooney before carbing up at The Cheesecake Factory.

The alarm went off at 3.30 a.m., and I showered and was ready to leave for the race start at 4 a.m. I didn't actually feel too tired given the lack of sleep. I made my way again through Downtown Disney (eating a bowl of porridge on the way) and dropped off my bag. The atmosphere at the race start area was good, and the energy was pumping despite the early start. When I arrived, the song playing was by the Spice Girls. Did they know I was coming? Fellow runners were a mixture of civilians in ordinary running gear (like me) and those that had been completely Disney-fied and had transformed into various Disney princesses and mostly Tinkerbell. I spotted one male runner in a T-shirt with the slogan "Evil Fairy", which made me very jealous.

We made our way to the start corals in the fairly pleasant temperature. The race was billed as a female-focused half marathon, meaning that there wasn't as much testosterone in the start pens as I am used to. I was in start wave B since the A group was reserved exclusively for woman. I spoke to fellow runners who had all run other Disney events previously. I can honestly say that the atmosphere was amongst the most friendly I have ever experienced. This truly was going to be a happy race in "the happiest place on Earth". My only slight worry was when one competitor asked me why I was running in the States. I explained about my challenge and said this was the time to give LA a turn. He apologized and said that he didn't like to disappoint me but we weren't actually in LA and that Disneyland is actually in the city of Orange County, so this wouldn't count. I humoured him whilst thinking to myself that in my eyes, it count as a run in LA, and for those who don't agree, I had already done a training run from West Hollywood into Beverly Hills (which incidentally I loved), so I had already covered an LA run if people decided not to accept this one.

Given my behaviour (in terms of alcohol consumption and lack of sleep) the previous few days, I wasn't going to be aiming for a PB. After all, it was only twenty-four hours earlier that I had gotten home from the Hamburger Mary's and West Hollywood drinking session, which clearly isn't on par with my normal race preparation. I was just ready to have fun on the run.

The ten-second countdown then started. We were off. Minnie Mouse and Daisy Duck (still on girl power theme of the event) waved us off as we crossed the line. The women in zone A had set off about eight to ten minutes before my group, and since I was at the front of my group, it meant that it was rather clear as we made our way along Disneyland Drive for the first mile. I was keeping a good pace, and there was only one runner in front of me. He was going quickly, so I had no intention of trying to catch him. As we passed mile one, I had already caught up with the zone A group. As I was going past, lots of the woman were saying, "Here come the men. Good job." This was secretly a bit of an ego boost.

We then entered the first of the two Disney parks and passed a few characters on the sidelines, which was fun. We went through the familiar themed lands and soon were passing down Main Street USA and through the famous Disney castle. Even the most manly of men (including me) would struggle not to find that part of the run exciting.

As we carried on past miles three and four, I noticed that I was actually catching up with the leading man. Soon I was then running next to him. I thought we would continue to run together, but after a few minutes, he started to fall behind. I carried on at my own pace, passing miles five and six, still overtaking the last few woman from the leading pack. As I reached mile seven, I was running on my own, with no runners in sight ahead of me and as far as I could tell none behind me either. At this point, we had left the actual Disney parks and were running on the surrounding streets, which were (as all things American) huge boulevards. There were pockets of supporters, which felt great to run past, as it felt like my own personal fans. I high-fived a lot of them as I went past to say thanks for being up so early and having the energy to cheer at six in the morning.

So I was running alone, bar the official who was cycling next to me. I was the leader of the men's race. As we passed each mile, I could hear him radio in saying "Lead male passing mile eight" and quoting the official clock time as I passed the marker. This happened at miles eight, nine, ten, eleven, twelve, and thirteen. I really wanted to finish in first place out of the males. I had said to myself at the start that I wasn't interested in doing a good time, but when you had led a race for that long, it would be devastating to lose out in the last few hundred metres.

As I was nearing the end, the man on the bike told me it was just around the corner and I was home. I pushed on through and noted the crowds lined up either side of the last stretch of the race. The cheers were welcomed, and I was glancing from side to side to see Sophie, Claire, and Laura, but I didn't catch them before crossing the line. Just as I did, I heard the commentator say, "Michael Long from London coming home in first place out of the men," which was amazing to hear. I had finished in second place overall but first out of all the men. Not a bad feat out of sixteen thousand people in all. My finish time was one hour, twenty-one minutes, and twenty-seven seconds. Even though not a PB, I was happy. Perhaps it was the fairy wings on my trainers that brought me home in second place.

I then looked for the girls. How did I miss them at the end? It turns out that it was because they weren't there! The cheek of coming on the holiday without coming to see the race and especially when I had finished second … To be fair to them, they had set off to come and see the finish but had gotten stuck in the people traffic in Downtown Disney. Thus they had just missed me. Plus, they thought there was a small earthquake as they waited to get across one road, so I let them off, though I did have to ask them if it was really an earthquake or just the speed of my running.

Post-run I enjoyed a massage and then a bit of people watching as the masses came in over the finish line. It was great to see so many achieving their first half marathon finish, although one girl had the worst chafing I have ever seen. Let's just say that her inner thighs were dripping with blood. Not a pretty sight, but she didn't seem fazed by it at all.

So a great race in a great place. Sadly, they only gave out awards to the top three woman and not the men, which was a shame. I know it was a woman-focused race, but since it did allow men to take part, it would have been a nice nod to acknowledge the men – but there we go. I was still happy, plus an afternoon in Disneyland itself beckoned.

One thing I did notice after the race was that my pee was a rose colour. I knew this meant that I was pretty dehydrated. I drank lots of water to refuel and knew that whilst being fun, my race preparation was not optimal for such a long race. Lesson learnt; don't overkill on alcohol and soft drinks in the lead-up to a half marathon.

So after a fun day in Disneyland (where in total for the day I had racked up almost forty kilometres on my feet), we made our way to Venice Beach for a few days of relaxing. It was a perfect way to finish off our week in LA. People watching, beachside beers, oceanfront cycling on tandems, and a run along the beach allowed me to say that I was "So Cal", as they say in the Golden State.

It was a fantastic trip and a great race result. So that was my nineteenth Olympic city crossed off the list. That means there were only four left to go. Part of me was starting to feel sad that the challenge was coming to an end. I was already panicking about what I was going to do after this was all finished. How was I going to stay out of trouble once I didn't have this to plan and keep me occupied? But I had time to think about that. There were still four more cities to get through yet.

Target: 23
Completed: 19

Chapter 22

Atlanta – I'm pregnant

Olympic year: 1996
Atlanta Olympic fact: Michael Johnson was the first person to
win gold in the both the 200m and 400m events in one games.
The world record he set in the 200m stood for 12 years.

When the decision was being made as to where to hold the 1996 Summer Olympic Games, it should have been clear. It was to be the centenary of the modern Olympic Games, and in my opinion, they should have been awarded to Athens, where the games began. Athens had bid to host the games in '96 and living there at the time (albeit as a youngster) I still was very much in full support of the bid and often wore my bid support T-shirt. Somehow, my T-shirt attire seemed to evade the attention of the IOC and the games were awarded to Atlanta. I was gutted.

Nonetheless, I still supported the games in Atlanta and watched them when they were on. The biggest memories of the games include Michael Johnson and his odd-looking running style; the bomb in the Olympic village; Michelle, the Irish swimmer who came out of nowhere and won lots of gold (since taken back due to doping); and Gloria Estefan singing the official song "Reach". What a tune.

So as I started to plan when I could do a run in Atlanta, it dawned on me that three of the four cities I had left to run in (Atlanta, St. Louis, Mexico City, and Rio) were located in North America. What about doing one trip and taking them all in rather than flying across the pond numerous times? Coincidentally, I was nearing my tenth anniversary of working at Expedia Inc., and I made the bullish move of asking my manager to give me one month off work to celebrate this fact. She agreed. In fact, she said that she thought I was going to ask for three to six months off. Oh. Never mind – I still got the result I wanted.

The planning began. I found a half marathon in St. Louis during the month I had off and snapped up my place quickly. For Atlanta and Mexico City, I was going to have to be creative with the events I did, as I couldn't find any official ones that would fit in with the dates. No matter. I had done that before and could do it again. So here was the plan for the month, beginning with a road trip across the United States:

Dallas
Austin
New Orleans
Memphis
Nashville
Pigeon Forge (Dollywood, if I'm honest)
Atlanta
St. Louis

Then a couple of weeks in sunny Mexico, visiting Cancun and Mexico City.

Quite a trip. None of the cities disappointed, and despite the initial shock of how much fried food there was on offer in the South, I managed to stay in shape with the help of hotel treadmills. Having said that, a few days into the trip, my foot started to feel a little sore. Was it the treadmill running? Was it the walking around cities sightseeing all day? I am not sure, to be honest, but the remedy would be a few days off training. Ask any runner and this is certainly an unnatural state of affairs. No matter how much I know that rest is sometimes is required, it still pains me (more than the sore foot) to take time out of my training schedule. However, I was very good and did so. The result: my foot was fine and would allow me to keep running in Atlanta.

For my run in Atlanta, I had researched city running tours like the one I had done in Rome. Bingo. There was one available, and the woman who ran them (another intended pun) said I just needed to contact her shortly before travelling and we could do a ten-kilometre tour around the city together.

Three weeks before setting off on my trip, I emailed her to see if the deal still stood. An immediate response confirmed she would have loved to but she was now heavily pregnant and therefore wasn't doing any tours. Yikes. What to do? She kindly put in me touch with a local running specialist shop called Big Peach Running Tours. They did weekly runs that anybody could turn up to and join in for free. Excellent – I was back on track. After a short email conversation with them, it turned out that the night I planned to arrive in Atlanta, they were due to do a six-mile run around the city and I was more than welcome to join.

I was confused by the running shop's name, but it transpires (after a quick Google) that the state of Georgia is known as the Peach State due to the importance of the peach business to its economy. Who knew?

On arrival in Atlanta, I had time for a quick shower and change, and then it was off to find the shop for my evening run. Once I got there, the man in charge (Dave) was super friendly and took me under his wing. He asked what pace I would like to run at and introduced me to an equally friendly chap called Nick, who would be running at the same pace. Brilliant – I could stick with him and not worry about getting lost. Dave gave me a map and directions for the run, but since I had only been in the city a couple of hours, my navigation knowledge consisted of the hotel and the running shop, which were on the same (albeit long) street; therefore, my confidence of leading the run was not high.

Dave then welcomed the group and introduced me to the others as Mike from London. Cardinal sin calling me Mike. Perhaps my face said it all, as he quickly corrected himself and then introduced me as Michael from London. Cue a high five from the woman next to me. I love America.

So we set out into the city. The route took us through the suburbs and parks on the outskirts of downtown, where we had begun. The park and the houses that we passed were magnificent. We ran through the gay district, where a couple of the pedestrian crossings had been painted in rainbow colours, which I loved, and even passed a few churches that were displaying the pride flag in aid of pride, which was taking place in the city later in the month. Very welcoming of the churches to do so.

As we looped back to return to the CBD (Central Business District), the view was fantastic. As dusk was upon us, the silhouettes of the skyscrapers lining the horizon were a brilliant sight to see, and I wished I had gotten better photos of it. Nick and another gentlemen called Larry were going at a good pace and leading the pack, but it did mean the photo opportunity stops were non-existent. I managed to get a few of the city and also a shaky one of the two of them just ahead of me, for I thought it would be good to remember the view I had of them leading me through the city. What I didn't count on was that at that moment of taking the photo, I almost trod on a cat that had been the victim of a hit-and-run driver. Fortunately, I didn't have to take the role of the guy who trod on the dead cat when we got back to the store. Nobody wants to be him.

As we neared the last mile, Nick and I were slightly ahead of Larry and I heard him say something but couldn't make out what. A few seconds later, Nick shouted, "See you later, Larry!" He then turned off to make his way straight home. I felt terrible because he probably thought I was incredibly rude not saying anything before he turned the corner, but the moment (and he) was now gone. If you ever read this, Larry, thanks for leading me around the city, and bye!

Atlanta had been quite hilly and the evening was quite humid whilst running, so the water and refreshments at the shop when we got back were welcome. Everyone hung out (as Americans say) for a little while, although I was too embarrassed to ask them to take a picture of me with my American flag for the blog and book. A selfie in their bathroom would have to do. I asked Nick where would be a good place to go for dinner and some drinks that evening. His response shocked me. "I'm not twenty-one yet, so I can't go into bars yet, but I hear there are good ones on this street." OMFG. That means he was only one when the Olympics took place in the city.

That aside, his advice rang true and I found some very nice places to eat and drink (because I am firmly over the age of twenty-one) that night to celebrate.

Atlanta had a nice park downtown to celebrate the Olympics; however, there were many Olympic artefacts in the World of Coca-Cola museum. Coke have been a sponsor of the Olympics since 1928 (the Amsterdam Games), so there were many pins and pictures in the museum, which was a fun addition to my weekend in the city.

It wasn't a difficult or even timed run in Atlanta, but it still counts as my Atlanta chapter, I think.

Thanks, Big Peach, for ensuring I had a run to do and for not getting pregnant!

Target: 23
Cities completed: 20

P.S. Just a quick amusing anecdote from the trip to share that has nothing to do with running. All the hotels I stayed in were amazing. Apart from one, that is. Arriving in Austin, the satnav seemed to be saying we were nearing our destination, right by the motorway. "Pull over on the left," I said to Steven, "and we can check that I put the right address in."

On the left was a Days Inn Hotel, so Steven pulled in. Sure, we were due to stay at a Days Inn but it must be a coincidence, no? The hotel was a typical American motel (i.e., it was set around a car park). We went into the reception to be greeted by a large woman with numerous tats. She was called Precious. I'm not lying. We asked if there was a reservation under the name of Puzey. "No," she said. We breathed a sigh of relief.

"Just to check, you don't have one under the name of Long do you, I enquired? Michael?"

"I sure do, but your room is not ready to check in yet."

Shit. We were indeed due to be staying here. Oh well, it was only for two nights, and we would literally be there to sleep. How bad could the room be? Pretty bad, as we found out. A dubious red stain on the wall, unmade bed, and a bath made for leprechauns were some of the highlights. However, it got better, and I share this with you purely to make you laugh.

After a day in the superb city that is Austin, Steven, Karen, and I came back to the pit that was the Days Inn University. The swimming pool was tiny, located right next to the highway, and surrounded by a fence. I thought, *A pool this crappy has to be swum in just for shits and giggles.* I donned my trunks and headed down to the car park and across to said pool to find it was locked. I made my way to reception, where Precious told me the pool was shut due to a chemical imbalance. Interesting excuse. Perhaps it was still being cleaned from when the body that had presumably been killed in my room (you remember the red stains upon check-in) was dumped in the pool.

As a swim was not in the cards, I made my way back across the car park to my room, only to be greeted by an evil pit bull–type dog. I tried to pretend it was going to be friendly, but it growled, snarled, and showed its teeth. I began to shit myself a little. I didn't know what to do standing there in my tiny Bjorn Borg trunks in the car park. Cue Precious to the rescue. She came out of reception and chased the dog away. Phew. Two starts out of five for the hotel and ten out of five for the reception staff.

I got back to the room, where Steven and Karen said in their strong Aussie accents, "You don't look very wet," to which I regaled what had just happened.

"We heard a dog barking and wondered what was going on."

Well, at least Precious had cared enough to check, eh? I am forever in debt to her.

Chapter 23

St. Louis – I Love Rock 'n' Roll

Olympic year: 1904
St. Louis Olympic fact: The games were
originally awarded to Chicago.

I landed in Las Vegas for a weeklong work conference in December 2011 to find out that the following day was the Rock 'n' Roll Las Vegas half marathon. I was gutted because had I known it was taking place, I definitely would have entered. In hindsight, it was a good thing I was not running the next day, for that evening turned into a rather impromptu evening of shots, dancing, and general death by minibar, which is no way to prepare for a race. However, the following year, I returned to Las Vegas for the weekend primarily to run the race. The night before was still a late one (as they always are in Vegas), but it was much more civilized in the form of seeing a Cirque du Soleil show, followed by a late dinner and ice cream.

The Rock 'n' Roll Vegas run is actually a night-time run and goes up and down the Strip. It's a fantastic route, allowing you to take in the bright lights of the strip as well as the downtown area. Many bands line the route, hence the rock 'n' roll title the event affords. It was a great race to be in, and I finished it in one hour, thirty-one minutes, and thirty-five seconds, which is not bad given I had flown there all the way from London for only two nights to take part! I would love to return to this event, as they now have an option for you to do a "run thru wedding", where you can marry a fellow competitor along the way. Sounds great to me. Any takers? No? OK, let's move on.

After this, I then began to see rock 'n' roll runs pop up all over the place, and I then ran one of the inaugural ones in Edinburgh (in one hour and twenty-seven minutes) and Liverpool (one hour, twenty-one minutes, and one second), which were also great events (although no wedding option included). The medals are some of the best race bling you will ever get. So I wanted to compete in a rock 'n' roll race as part of my Olympic challenge. Enter St. Louis.

After the road trip which took in Atlanta (from the chapter before), I made my way to St. Louis for a couple of days for the half marathon. I didn't really know much about the city, apart from the fact it had an impressive monumental arch (630 feet tall, for those interested) and was featured in the Judy Garland musical movie *Meet Me in St. Louis*. I landed and headed straight for race registration. It was a simple process and got me excited for the race. I checked into my hotel and then made my way down to the Mississippi River to see both the arch and go on an old-fashioned boat (called *Tom Sawyer* no less).The city was much more urban than I thought it would be. By that, I mean that the factories and old buildings that lined the streets and the river gave it a raw feel. I liked it. It made for some excellent pictures, particularly in black and white.

The night before the event was actually a bit of a strange one for me. As an extremely seasoned traveller, I rarely have experienced homesickness, but all I could think of is that this is what I had. I guess going from two weeks on the road with the boyfriend to then being on your own (also in the lead-up to the first anniversary of the passing of your mum) is possibly conducive to suddenly feeling a little deflated. I had a quick word with myself and ordered room service to carb up, enjoying a couple of classic movies from bed in what was a lovely hotel room.

I awoke at 5 a.m. feeling refreshed and ready to race. The night before, I had bought some bananas and a single bowl of porridge which you add water to for my breakfast. This did not turn out to be the breakfast of champions that I had envisaged. Sadly, the pot ended up being a rather waterlogged wheat bowl mess, but I still ate it. Needs must on a race day.

I left my hotel room to discover a clearly intoxicated woman asleep against the ice machine in the hallway. I asked her if she was OK, and she said yes. Did she not realize she probably would be more comfortable in her actual room? Before leaving the hotel, I let the receptionist know that there was a woman asleep in the corridor of the eighth floor. Before I finished my sentence, he said he knew about the woman on the tenth floor. Oh dear. I wondered if it was the same woman and she had moved or if there were two of them. I'll have to live never knowing the truth. I am sure that is doable.

I then made my way through the dark morning (or should that be night?) to the start line. I had paid for entrance into the VIP area, which had promised our own bag drop, immediate access to the start pens, sustenance before the race, sustenance post-race, massage, and our own set of toilets. I was easily sold on this and only wish it were a service offered by all races. I would sign up every time. It was freezing, but I could stand in one of our tents to shelter slightly. I then realized that they were actually serving great porridge (or oatmeal, as it is known stateside).

#devastated

If I had realized that, I wouldn't have filled up on gruel before arriving. Oh well, time to get on with the rest of my usual race prep. About ten minutes before heading to the start line, I thought I would take my usual pre-race pee break. I made my way to our VIP toilets. No queue. Completely clean. This made a lovely change. It was still dark, though, and with no lighting in the cubicles, it would make for an interesting aim. Feeling resourceful, I turned to the torch on my phone. Marvellous. Although as I aimed the torch in the necessary direction to ensure a good shot at the urinal, I realized that if the walls were transparent it would look like I was taking a dick pic. As the urine left my body, I could see the steam rising in the light of the torch. It was definitely cold then and not the ideal temperature to take a flattering dick pic. Of course not that I was considering it, you understand.

We then lined up in our corrals. We faced towards the arch just as the sun was beginning to break over the top. It looked stunning. I always forget that each race in the United States starts with the national anthem. As it was sung by a local singer, all the athletes around me stood with their hand on their hearts (not in the Kylie Minogue fashion, sadly). I realized it sort of looked like I was joining in, as I had my hands under my armpits to keep warm. Perhaps I just looked as if I had gotten it slightly wrong, like when George W. Bush once stood with his hand on his stomach (Google Image it).

Almost time for the race to begin. Just one last moment for the official videographer to ask four of us to look at him and shout, "Here we go! St. Louis rocks!" We did it, and for some reason, I adopted an American accent. Why? I have no idea. Perhaps because shouting that something "rocks" in an English accent just doesn't quite sound, right?

Across the line we went. I seemed to be in third position. *This can't be right*, I thought. That's because it wasn't. Soon enough, there were people passing me. I wasn't put out by this, as I was intent on enjoying the race and seeing the city. Above all, I wanted to warm up.

As I mentioned, the city has a real urban feel, and I really liked this. There are not the high skyscrapers that you get in other US cities (because nothing can be higher than the arch), and it reminded me of how I viewed the United States when I was young, based off eighties movies. We passed some fantastic old-fashioned theatres and then went into an area called The Grove. It boasted fantastic street art, rainbow pedestrian crossings, and some unique-looking shops. I made a note to myself of the street names in order to come back and have a wander the next day because it looked so quirky.

I was slightly warmer at this point, but my thumbs were still chilly, despite running with them tucked into my clenched fists. As we rounded another corner, I was hit with the sun. It felt gorgeous on my skin and had me thinking that this was going to be the point where I would cease resembling Olaf from *Frozen*. The long stretch ahead was uphill and into the direct sunlight, but I didn't care that I couldn't see where I was going. I felt warm. Plus, maybe it was a blessing not knowing how much longer the hill would go on. A mile or so later, I summited the hill and was back into more shady (in terms of temperature) areas. We passed through a beautiful park, saw amazing houses, and soon were on the home stretch back to the CBD. But not before we passed a big sign which read "WTF ... Where's the finish line?" It made me smile.

We were running along huge empty boulevards, and being close to the front of the pack, it almost felt I had the city to myself. Around one last corner, I could see the magnificent arch again. I crossed the line in one hour, twenty-four minutes, and two seconds. It was by no means a personal best, but I was happy to have completed my twenty-first Olympic city run, and it turned out I still placed twenty-fifth overall, which was great.

I was still chilly (and sweat-free, which shows how cold it was), so I made my way back to the VIP tent for a massage, lovely food, and a pee in a clean portaloo (this time without the use of a torch, but I did sneak in a quick dick pic. I'm kidding).

As I put on my tracksuit (words a fashionista never likes to say out loud or in print), one spectator said, "I'm cold just looking at you. Would you like to borrow some of my body fat?" A kind offer, I thought, but I politely declined.

Back at the hotel, I had a lovely warm shower and returned to a healthy pink colour. That evening, I made my way to happy hour at the hotel bar and enjoyed drinks and a pizza with other guests. I retired to bed rather early once the hotel had given me a cookie and warm milk after dinner. I had been up at five that morning after all.

So there you have it. City number twenty-one completed. Judy Garland's ghost didn't come to meet me, but I still had a great time in the city and I still love rock 'n' roll races. Bring on the next one. Maybe Lisbon?

Target: 23
Completed: 21

Chapter 24

Mexico City – I Think You May Have a Drinking Problem

Olympic year: 1968
Mexico City Olympic fact: Many athletes achieved world record times, but they didn't count due to the city being at such a high altitude, thus giving an advantage because of the thin air.

I truly was nearing the end of this challenge. Only two cities left to go. Yikes.

After an amazing couple of weeks in the United States (with a renewed playlist featuring a lot of Elvis, Dolly Parton, and other country music) I was bound for Mexico. I had only ever been to the country for the day before, so I was excited to see more of it. It sounds rather decadent saying I had only been for the day, but it's not as uncommon as it sounds. I was once staying in San Diego and decided to hop south of the border for the day to visit nearby Tijuana. It was a great trip, with the best Mexican food I had ever tasted and possibly the busiest border crossing back into the United States that

I have ever seen. This time immigration was not as crowded, and I exited the airport to the tropical heat of Cancun (and a Margaritaville cocktail stand in the car park).

Resisting the temptation for an early margarita, I made my way to the hotel and awaited Laura's arrival from London. The hotel was set right upon the beach, and our balcony looked out over the ocean. It was a perfect view. This is perhaps why it was dubbed a "romantic" room, which would regretfully be wasted (in that sense) on two friends sharing.

Cancun was a perfect place to relax. The beach is stunning, and each morning (or sometimes evening) I would run for forty minutes barefoot along the shore. It certainly beat the treadmills of the past few weeks. We enjoyed day trips to the amazing Chichen Itza and Tulum and of course took advantage of the poolside bar. We then left the beach and spent a couple of nights in the jungle, which was splendid. Complete silence and time to just completely relax (and get bitten to shit by the local mosquitoes).

So then it was on to Mexico City. Flying in was spectacular. The city did indeed look massive, and thus I was expecting it to live up to the "crazy busy" reputation it seems to hold. The airport was calm and as one would expect, with immigration the same. Our airport transfer was ready and waiting for us as anticipated. Were we in the right place? I will admit the traffic on the way to our hotel was busy but no worse than that I have experienced in London. I think Mexico City gets a bad rep as a busy and dangerous city, and here is where I will start to tell you how different my experience of this wonderful city was.

We were staying in La Rosa area, which is just off the main avenue Reforma. There was great architecture along the avenue, and I swear I didn't know that this was the gay area of town when I booked my hotel. There were some lively bars and trendy shops on our street (as any self-respecting gay area would have), and that meant that when I returned to treadmill training in the gym, I could play my Kylie playlist loud and proud on the music system. Not that I wouldn't normally be proud of this playlist – just that it would almost be expected in this part of town.

Over the coming days, we enjoyed great museums (the anthropology museum is one of the best I have visited), excellent food (the best seared tuna I have ever had), a stunning old town and main square, an afternoon in the house of the incredibly talented Frida Khalo, as well as history in the form of more pyramids in the city of Teotihuacan, on the outskirts of the city. We enjoyed a meal with a local family and found the hospitality of the Mexican people beyond friendly. We felt safe in the city and became experts at the metro system. This city should be on everyone's to-do list. I promise you won't regret it.

But on to the running piece. What race was I going to do? There wasn't an official race happening when I was in the city, and whilst my Kylie gym sessions were a fun way to start the day, I don't think it could count as an Olympic run, do you? So I researched for local running clubs again and came across the Hash House Harriers. I had heard of the club way back when I was a child living in Greece, but I had never run with them before. Their website describes themselves as a "drinking club with a running problem", which had me sold. I was in. I dropped them an email, and shortly afterwards, Mario (the leader of the Mexico City group) responded (from his email address, which was Mario the Frog), saying he would love to host me and we could do a bespoke run on the Sunday I was in town. He asked for details of what I wanted to do so that he could put it up on their website in both English and Spanish. Lovely guy.

It was going to be the Day of the Dead celebrations that weekend I was in Mexico City, so I said that if we could run somewhere to take in the atmosphere, that would be great. True to his word, he put the description of what I wanted to do on his website and confirmed that we would be doing a ten-kilometre run together that day. What I wasn't sure of was what he meant by *we*. Was that him and me or would others be involved as well? Only time would tell.

As the Sunday drew nearer, I emailed Mario to check that we were still on and see where we should meet. He gave me the address of the club's headquarters and said that I should be there at 11.30. I misread this as 10.30, so I arrived one hour early. Bet early than late, I suppose. He also said just to bring myself as well as a gift in the form of alcohol. I bought a bottle of wine and had it in my rucksack, wondering whether I was going to have to run with it for the entire ten kilometres or whether he would take it off my hands before we left. Fortunately, it turned out to be the latter; otherwise, that would have been a heavy and clinking load to carry.

Mario let me into the huge house and took me up to a splendid roof garden. The sun was shining, and we sat down to enjoy a nice coffee. A couple of things I noticed about his décor was that there were frog ornaments everywhere (the email address made sense now) and that there were two small skeletons hanging in the centre of the garden, which he said represented his mum and dad, who were no longer with us. As I would find out over the next twenty-four hours, the Mexicans really do have a different way to celebrate the dead and to remember them. I thought this was a nice gesture.

Mario was sixty-five, and as well as running the Hash House Harriers, he had once been the head of security for the US embassy in Mexico City. The walls inside the house were covered with photos and letters from US presidents and other members of government, thanking him for his hospitality during their visits to his city. Since retiring, he rented out his spare rooms in the house to women who were in need of short-term accommodation and were looking for a safe place on a budget. In addition to his interesting career, he mentioned on numerous occasions that "I was once in a relationship with the Finnish ambassador". Not sure why I needed to know but I like it when people feel they can be an open book with me. He was indeed quite a character.

As he prepared things for our run later that day, one of the women (Lupita) who lived in the house sat with me to talk about her studies and her passion for art. Until I arrived, she had been painting in the rooftop garden, and the result (to date) was something I would have had happily on my walls at home. A talented girl. Unfortunately, she wouldn't be joining us on the run, as she had dropped a glass on her foot a few days before and thus wasn't able to put weight on her foot, but she said she would join us in town later on for some food.

So far, then, there was just Mario and me running. Would there be others? Shortly before 11.30, a group of three arrived. Our group was growing! The oldest male was Fidel, and his son and daughter were twenty and eighteen respectively. They were all very friendly, and we managed to communicate with my broken Spanish and their basic knowledge of English. Sign language always comes in handy, as we all know. At 11.30, two other people, Ricco and Cay, arrived. Our group was now complete.

We all sat in the garden, and Mario formally introduced himself and described the route we would be taking. We would take the metro to the north of the city, where we would walk for about twenty minutes to a park. Then we would jog up to a cemetery, where we could see people celebrating Day of the Dead, before jogging back down the hill into the city to catch the metro to the city centre to meet Lupita (as well as her mother and younger sister) for a late lunch. Sounded awesome to me.

He then asked us to introduce ourselves. The introductions were as you would expect – I'm Michael, and I'm from London – but as I gave mine, both Ricco and Cay said in unison, "So you're just Michael." This puzzled me and had me thinking that perhaps I should have been more formal and included my last name. Oh well, the moment had now passed. However, then it was their turn to introduce themselves. Here is what they said:

"I'm Ricco 'two inches in ladyboy.'"

"And I'm Cay 'Dr yoga sew UR sak.'"

They said they usually run with the Baghdad Hash House Harriers.

Two questions arose from me. Firstly, there was a running club in Baghdad? Secondly, what did those nicknames mean?

And so they told me.

They were working in the army and had both been based in Iraq for the last three years, where they had met at the running club and since gotten married. They had transferred to Mexico City only that week, so they were newbies to the city. The names apparently are given to you once you are a fully-fledged member of any Hash House Harriers. The naming ceremony can vary, but in Iraq it transpired that they sat you on a block of ice blindfolded and asked you personal questions until they had enough information to give you a "Hash name". Until that time, you were known as "just" and your name, hence why I was "just Michael" to them. Made sense to me, but given what you had to go through to get your hash name, I was quite happy to stick with "just" for now. It worked for Jack in *Will and Grace*, so it was good enough for me.

So off we set. Mario knew the city well, and during our first walk, he pointed out some interesting buildings and a monument that was on a site where a light aircraft crashed onto a busy market and killed various people. We then started jogging. It was light going, but that was fine. It was nice for us to stay as a group. As we reached a pedestrian flyover, he told us we could run quickly up it. I took his word and did so, feeling lightheaded about halfway up. This was the first (and admittedly only) time that I felt I was at that altitude.

We then arrived at the graveyard. It was busy. Not busy with quiet mourners but busy with food and flower sellers and hundreds of people who had come to celebrate the dead. As we jogged through the cemetery, there were families having picnics at their family graves. They had balloons, drinks, music, and were enjoying each other's company as they sat around, presumably remembering those they had lost. It was poignant but lovely to see people remembering others in such a fond way. Cemeteries are typically a place for peaceful reflection, but not that day – or in Mexico, it seemed.

We passed many children's graves which had parents gathered around hosting what would have looked like a birthday party had it not been for the obvious setting. We saw a grave to mark the forty thousand people who were killed in the earthquake of 1985. Mario, who also lost his home in the earthquake, said that the government only acknowledged that four thousand people perished in the quake. I am not sure why releasing the actual number of people killed would weaken Mexico's image worldwide; however, since researching the quake since my trip, it does seem the lower number is what is reported.

We were then serenaded by an elderly gentleman with some local mariachi music just before making our way out of the cemetery. It was an experience like no other and was the beginning of how I would change looking at death.

We continued our gentle jog down the hills through some exclusive areas of the city. The houses were enormous, with plenty of expensive cars parked in front of them. This part of town could easily be confused with Beverly Hills if I were to show you a picture of it. Mario (of course) had attended diplomatic parties in many of the houses and said that each house had a huge security team. This was the first time since being in the city that I had even a hint that there was any more danger than in any other global capital, but I didn't feel any danger myself.

Running through these forests was really peaceful and totally different to what I had expected of my Mexico City run. Mario, Fidel, and I were up at the front of the group, and despite Cay and Ricco having aired worries of the group not being fast enough at the beginning of the jog, they had fallen behind and were at the tail with Fidel's children. Ironic that those who were out for a quick sprint and the youngest of the group were at the back or, as Mario put it, "Fidel was a front-running bastard." All in good jest, you understand.

As we neared the old part of the city, we reached the crowds, who by now were all donning the traditional face paints of the Day of the Dead celebrations. It was a fantastic atmosphere, and we met Lupita and her family in a local restaurant, where Mario had told me that as long as you order a drink, then the food was free. I figured this sentence was being lost in translation, but true to his word, when the bill came, I indeed was only paying for a couple of beers and the three courses I had been brought were free. No wonder this was his favourite place to replenish the burned calories post-Sunday runs. Mario washed down his dinner with straight tequila, which he said his doctor had told him would be good for his cholesterol levels. Not sure if that was true or whether Mario just had the same doctor as Patsy from *Ab Fab*.

From talking to Ricco and Cay, this was very different to the normal Hash House Harrier run in that it was a lot slower than usual and there was far less drinking than they were used to, but I still enjoyed it and I hope it stays that way whilst Mario runs the group.

So there was no timing and no official distance in this jog across the city, but it was indeed a fun one and it holds a dear place in my heart. After I left the group, I experienced the night-time version of Day of the Dead in an equally lively cemetery in the south of the city. I am unable to describe how it felt. All I can say is that it has altered the way I would like to celebrate my parents' lives, which I will do on 1 November every year from now on.

Thanks, Mexico City, for offering me more than just a run. One day I will return, I promise.

Target: 23
Completed: 22

P.S. For those interested in the meaning of Ricco's and Cay's Hash names, here you go. "Two inches in ladyboy" was apparently from when Ricco had to defend a ladyboy against a drunk with a two-inch-long knife. I have a feeling the truth would reveal a different story, don't you? And "Dr yoga sew UR sak" is because Cay is a doctor who likes yoga. She once conducted an operation on a man's leg whose sack was so large it became an obstruction and the only way for her to complete the operation was to sew his sack against his own leg. Nice. So there you have it. I still think I will stick with "just Michael".

Chapter 25

Rio de Janeiro – In Search of the Showgirl

Olympic year: 2016
Mexico City Olympic fact: These were the
first games held in Latin America.

I couldn't quite believe I was on to the final city. Taking stock of what I had achieved so far, it really did feel a little surreal. Technically, I had already raced in every Summer Olympics city, as the games in Rio were not due to take place until August 2016 and I was heading out for my race in Rio in January of that year.

I had never been to Latin America, and running in Rio gave me the perfect excuse to visit a few places that had been on my wish list since I was a youngster. I had a two-week trip coming up, which consisted of Rio, the mighty Iguassu Falls on the border of Brazil and Argentina, Buenos Aires, and a short hop over to Colonia in Uruguay. I was beyond excited. It may not have seemed so because I portray more of a shout-about-it-inside kind of excitement, but believe me when I say that I was eager to get underway.

First stop Rio. I had a few days to explore the city before my race, and a splendid few days they were. I was staying at a hotel directly on Copacabana Beach. I challenge you to say the name of the beach without bursting into the Barry Manilow number. Couldn't do it, could you? Well, maybe you could and that is the gay in me coming out (again). That aside, I began each morning in Rio with a run along the beach. The promenade is fantastic and full of runners, cyclists, and pedestrians at all times of the day. The main road was actually closed on Sundays so that the public could use it traffic-free all the way along the beach. It was bloody marvellous, and with the huge waves and amazing mountains (including the world-famous Sugar Loaf Mountain) in constant view, it was a real treat to be able to run this way. It was a perfect way to people watch and take in sights of toned men (thanks for those, Brazil), a large woman in a G-string (no need for that, Brazil), and a woman chasing her pet chicken across the road, which seemed to be trying to provide an answer to the age-old question of why the chicken crossed the road.

The city itself was fantastic. I visited the colourful Lapa Steps, climbed to the top of Sugar Loaf Mountain (OK, I'll admit I got the cable car with everyone else), and took the train up the mountain to Christ the Redeemer (where I inappropriately muttered "Jesus Christ" to myself when getting frustrated with the gift shop being overrun with tourists), which dominates the skyline and sees every man and his dog taking selfies with JC himself. I am also now one of those people. It was all splendid and sums up why this city truly is world class and deserved of Olympic status.

I am not lying when I say that my mouth dropped open at some of the views I was able to take in, none more so than from one of the favelas that I visited. One thing I will say is that this must be the only city in the world where the wealthier residents live lower down than the poorer. In the favela, I went to a bar that had what I can only describe as million-dollar views. In any other city, the location of the bar would be beyond premium and cost a fortune to reside in. In Rio, however, it remained a part of the favela and thus was surrounded by crowded and small houses for those with limited means.

Enjoying a piña colada (which in Brazil seems to have the additional ingredient of chocolate, which I am not too sure about) on the terrace of said bar, I was in awe of not only the coastline and natural beauty but the organized chaos of the favela below. Due to the steep climb up the hillside, there are motorcycle cabs at the bottom of the village to take people up to the top. Rumour has it that when Rihanna was in town, she organized a drinks party in the same bar that I was in but had not been able to reach it because her car was ambushed with fans when they discovered it was her. Allegedly, she returned to the bottom, put on a crash helmet, and got a motorbike cab up to the bar without anyone even batting an eye. I did not have the same problem as Rihanna, and my car made it up to the top with no fans stopping me. However, perhaps my status in Brazil was due to change and the story in three days' time would be totally different.

The race I had entered was called Corrida de Sao Sebastio. I had read about it in the ultimate runs to do around the world. Runners could choose between a five-kilometre or ten-kilometre route, and it was held on Wednesday, 20 January, a public holiday to celebrate Sao Sebastio. Made sense. I entered the ten-kilometre race, and a couple of days ahead of time, I made my way to packet pickup in downtown Rio. The journey there was easy on the metro, and I found the office building I needed quickly enough.

One thing I'd instantly loved about Rio was the abundance of phone booths around the city. They were painted a lovely yellow and green and sported the phone network "Oi" on them. The ones outside the packet pickup office were less endearing, shall we say. Inside were countless stickers for call girls – ones with a difference. Let's just say chick with a dick and you can imagine the rest.

Packet pickup was straightforward, and I was all set for the race. The start time had been moved forward to 7.30am because it had been extremely hot in the previous weeks, although ironically it seemed the weather had now turned left at the traffic lights and was somewhat cloudy and rainy (although still around mid-twenties centigrade).

Prior to leaving London, the press office from the race had contacted me to ask why I was planning to compete in the race. I can only assume this was because I was either the only one or one of the few competitors with a listed address outside of Brazil. I explained to them about my challenge (secretly hoping they would want to do some PR), and they were thrilled to hear about it and were excited to welcome me to their event as my final race of the challenge. A few days later, they contacted me to say that they had arranged an interview for me with one of the largest newspapers in Brazil, called *O Globo*. Très exciting. I was told to meet the reporter in my hotel the Monday after I arrived. They said she was called Gabriella, was thirty, and had fair hair.

Dressed in my typical smart casual attire, I went for a coffee somewhere nearby so as not to be late back to the hotel. Returning to the hotel on time, I spotted a woman waiting in reception who was clearly over thirty, so I commented to Steven that it was definitely not the person waiting for me. At that time, the receptionist said, "Mr Long, this is Ana, and she is from *O Globo*. She is waiting for you." She was pointing straight at the woman I had just rebuffed as being the reporter. Oops. Turns out she wasn't the interviewer but the photographer and was going to be doing the shoot. Crumbs, I hadn't really thought we would be doing an official shoot, as the PR team had asked for previous race photos already. I thought they would use those. Nevertheless, it was going to add to the fun.

Ana was extremely nice, and shortly after our introductions, a guy called William arrived and said he would be doing the interview. Not sure what happened to Gabriella. Perhaps she was onto a much larger story. Both William and Ana commented how smart I looked but ideally wanted me to be wearing running gear for the photo they would eventually use in the paper. A quick dash up to my room and I was changed and ready to "run", so to speak. When I say "quick", I was indeed speedy, but I still did a quick fashion show (to myself in front of the bathroom mirror) in order to see which running top I looked best in. The City 2 Surf one from Sydney was the one that called to me.

Back with Ana and William, they explained to me that the interview would be on page two of the newspaper, in a column called "Tell Me Something I don't know". They were essentially unique stories (from non-famous people) to feature every day in the paper. It seemed that my challenge met the criteria. First up was the photo shoot.

Ana suggested we go to the rooftop pool of my hotel so we could do pictures overlooking Copacabana Beach. She wasn't convinced on the location since it has a glass balcony which would not have been conducive to clear pictures. So down we went to ground level and outside the hotel, where she wanted to do pictures of me in a running position in front of the stunning hotels that faced the Atlantic Ocean. Weirdly, I didn't feel self-conscious about the process of the shoot at all. As Ana lay on the pavement to get a good angle and directed me to look forward, at her, smile or not smile, it felt quite natural and fun. Watch your back, Kate Moss; there's a new basic bitch in town. After about five minutes, Ana said that she had all she needed and we were done. She said that usually it takes a lot longer than that but she was pleased with the shots. *Milan fashion week, here I come,* I thought.

Back inside the hotel, William then interviewed me for about forty-five minutes. He asked about the challenge, why I ran, why I thought other people ran, and if I noticed the difference in cultures in the cities in which I had run. He finished with the statement that marks the essence of page two: "Tell me something I don't know." Thinking on my toes the first story that came to mind was about the Streak for Tigers run, remember back in the London chapter? You haven't stopped thinking about it, I can tell. So the article came out and the title was "I have run naked and drunk in London zoo". I intend to adopt this as a sub title every time I make a first introduction to someone.

So race day was now upon us. It was an early start to get up, shower, and run to breakfast for a couple of bananas before hopping in a taxi to the start line. At this point, I still didn't know the course of the run, but I knew that we would be able to see Sugar

Loaf Mountain (should the mist disappear, that is). The start area was well set up, and the temperature at 6.45am was already twenty degrees centigrade. It wasn't particularly sunny, but the humidity was definitely up there. There were many running club tents (all of which Steven was hoping to get a free coffee from, but to no avail) and many runners who looked in good shape. I did a short warm-up and joined the crowds in the starting pen. On my way there, I noticed a man who looked to be in his seventies ready with his race number on and his timing chip tied around his ankle because he would be running barefoot. Crazy.

As we lined up, there was a man at the front carrying a ukulele and performing a little tune whilst we watched the elite woman depart ahead of us. Totally random race etiquette, but fun nonetheless.

Shortly after the woman had left, the elite men joined the pen ahead of us. As they gathered around, I thought they would be going first, followed by another start of the "masses" a minute or so after. However, as the horn went off, the elite men were off – and so it seemed were we. I was caught totally by surprise and was pulled along with the crowds across the start line. We were off!

The roads we were on were very wide, so I wasn't caught between many people, as can sometimes be the case, and within a few minutes, I was in my own rhythm. Ahead of me, I could see the one-kilometre mark. Surely not? As I passed it, I glanced at my watch to notice I had done the first kilometre in three minutes and twenty-one seconds. Way too fast, in fact, to maintain in those weather conditions. I carried on just enjoying the fact that we were running along the coast. It was beautiful even though the mist was blocking some of the view.

As we reached around 2.5 kilometres, we passed an amazing monument (to this day, I don't know what it's called but it did feature on the Olympic marathon route a few months later) and circled back towards the start. It was hot, and I was uber-sweaty. As we reached the five-kilometre mark, the road was divided into two (the left for those in the five-kilometre race and the right for the ten-kilometre racers). For the first time in my running career, I briefly wished I were doing the shorter distance. I had no choice, though – man up and carry on. The next few kilometres took us past Sugar Loaf Mountain (or "Sugar Tits", as Steven had come to affectionately refer to it) and up to a superb swimming pool which marked our second turning point. The stretch back to the finish was tough – I am not going to lie. The heat was something I was not used to, and the water stops couldn't come soon enough (entirely to pour on my head rather than drink, you understand).

As expected, I wasn't able to sustain my initial pace. I was averaging a four-minute kilometre now, which I was fine with. I wasn't aiming for a PB. The nine-kilometre marker passed me on my left, and I was on the home stretch. The finish line looked gorgeous when I saw it up ahead. The five-kilometre racers rejoined us on the left to cross the finish line, and over the line I went. My thirty-eight minutes and eleven seconds was just outside the thirty-eight-minute target I had wanted to beat (from about the halfway point). I placed thirty-fifth, which I was still pleased with given that the majority of finishers ahead of me were elite.

So that was that. My challenge was done. How did I feel? *Weird* is all I can say. I didn't cry (yet) or laugh. However, I did enjoy the watermelon and bananas they gave me (along with my final medal) at the finish. I did my finish photos by the sea and in the taxi back to the hotel reflected on what I had achieved. I was silently happy.

Before leaving for the race in the morning, I had posted on Facebook that only ten kilometres stood between me finishing my Olympic challenge. As I logged on when I got back to the room, I saw that I had hundreds of likes and numerous comments congratulating me already and saying I was an inspiration to my friends. I was so touched. As I said, I hadn't cried yet, but then I read one final comment. My friend congratulated me and said that wherever my parents were (having both passed away), they would be looking down on me bursting with pride. I couldn't hold it in, and I shed a few tears. I really do hope I have made them proud.

So there. I did cry at the end of the challenge, which I guess I should have, shouldn't I? I showered and made it back down to the breakfast room in the hotel in time for a late sitting. Bonus: they had champagne on the table. It was nice for Steven and me to raise a toast to what I had done.

That afternoon, we flew down to the Iguassu Falls to enjoy a few days in the national park, which was beyond spectacular. I can honestly say I have never seen anything like the falls before, especially when we took a speedboat to the foot of the falls. It was one of the most alive moments I have ever felt.

All too soon, my time in Brazil had ended, but I still had a week of holidays to look forward to, going to Argentina and Uruguay. An amazing trip, to say the least.

Leaving Brazil, I felt content and was looking forward to being able to watch the Olympics in a city I had just been to a mere seven months earlier.

So that was it. I was done.

Target: 23
Completed: 23

Epilogue: Was I Born to Run?

I never used to consider myself a runner or athlete, and all of this happened quite by accident, but now I can't contemplate my life without running.

Running gives me time to think about things that have happened in the day (both good and bad) and allows me time to relax. It may sound like a slightly bizarre way to unwind, but I genuinely would recommend it to anyone, as the feeling it gives both physically and mentally is the best, at least in my opinion.

This challenge has not only given me the motivation to stay fit, but I have also been lucky to travel to some of the most exciting cities on the planet. Whilst doing all of this, I have been able to catch up with some friends in most cities, thanks to Facebook informing me where people now live, despite not having had direct contact with them for decades in some cases. It truly has been an amazing adventure.

As a final piece to share with you, I was looking through old photos from my parents' albums (remember when we couldn't just digitally post pictures online but had to print them?) when I stumbled across the one below:

It's a picture of me in 1988, running in the stadium in Delphi, Greece. On the back, my mum had written "marathon man Michael", so perhaps this whole challenge was meant to be from a young age.

It's been fun. Now on to the next one. What to do?

Suggestions on a postcard, please. Or maybe just tweet me. May be quicker, eh?

The one I said I would tell you about later:

There's one last race I need to share, which was the London Marathon. Remember back at the beginning, when I said I would tell you later?

As you now know, I didn't manage to get under the three-hour mark in the Seoul Marathon; however, I was still determined to try to do that. Based on my result in Seoul, it meant that I had qualified for a "Good for Age" place, as I had run under the required three hour, five minute cut-off for men of my age group. So there was no excuse not to try to break my own PB. Plus, it made a nice end to this overall challenge – to actually finish it on home turf in London – particularly if I could break the three-hour mark.

The training plan had been set five months ahead of race day and was more aggressive than last time. There was a weekly hill session, some fast ten kilometres, some fast track sessions, and this time two long runs per week.

The long run on a Wednesday turned into my running home from work from Angel to Brentford. If you map this out, it is between fourteen and sixteen miles (dependent on the route), quite a lengthy training run after work. Nonetheless, I actually was enjoying it, and as the nights got lighter and we crept towards daylights saving, it was pleasant to be running along the Thames, past Westminster, the South Bank, and Chelsea.

Training had been going well, and I was on track to reach my goal. Race day was one week away, and I knew that if everything went perfectly on the day (such as weather, getting a good start, and so forth), then I could get a time of two hours, fifty-nine minutes, and fifty-nine seconds or less.

What I hadn't contemplated on was getting a cough a few days before. I rarely get ill, and having a tickle in my throat on the Friday night of race weekend, I put it down to nerves that the day was soon going to be here. Waking up on Saturday, it was clear this was no nervous tickle; a full chesty cough had developed. I was angry and upset. I had to go pick up my race number and did so via the pharmacy. I felt OK at the race expo but was so preoccupied by the thought of my cough getting worse that I wasn't getting that excited by the build-up of the race, only more anxious.

I was due to stay in a hotel at Tower Hill the night before the race, so I checked in there and enjoyed a nice long bath. By evening, I was actually feeling a little better and went out for the standard carb-loading meal.

That night, though, I didn't sleep well. I was up at least twice in the night to take more cough syrup and to clear my chest with an Olbas Oil face bath. I got up before my alarm even went off and was feeling a little deflated. In my head, I wasn't even sure if I would be able to run at all, let alone have a hope in hell of beating my PB. I ate breakfast and decided to make my way to the start line and see how I felt. I didn't say them out load, but I had two options. If I felt terrible when I got to the start, I would not do the race and speak to someone about deferring my place to the following year. If I felt OK, then I would begin running and just take it easy and enjoy the day.

Once I arrived at the start, the latter seemed to be the option I could go for (pretty sure a qualified doctor would have disagreed, though). I stayed warm in the changing tent until fifteen minutes before race time, when I lined up at the start. I still didn't have the excited feeling in my belly as I had during training because I still didn't know what I was going to feel like once I began to run.

The ten-second countdown started. We were off. The start was smooth, and I was into my rhythm very quickly. The crowds were lining the street from start to finish, and I have never experienced anything quite like it. It was loud, appreciated, and fun.

From miles one through to seventeen, I was keeping on track and had actually only coughed once. Perhaps the heavier breathing was actually clearing my lungs. I spotted various friends who had come to support me along the way, and each one had given me an extra boost. Crossing Tower Bridge was amazing, and despite most people speeding up at this point due to the insane crowds, I actually noticed that I slowed up as I took in the sights and sounds of what was around me. It was splendid.

After mile seventeen, though, I noticed that again my legs started to feel heavy. I pushed on through until around mile twenty-two, which was when I truly started slowing down. At this point, I had still only coughed twice, which was a miracle, but the three-hour pacemaker pulled in front of me. I tried to keep up with him for a few hundred metres, but then I realised if I did that for the next four miles, I would risk being really ill. I changed my goal in my head to make this the first marathon that I would run nonstop. The others had seen me walk a couple of times (albeit briefly) or stop to go to the loo, but this time I would make the entire 26.2 miles without a break. The last three miles were tough – I am not going to lie to you. The crowds were great, and the final approach up to Buckingham Palace was a real treat. I turned the corner and saw the sign saying there were only 365 yards to go.

I pushed on and crossed the line in three hours, three minutes, and twenty-five seconds. It was still a PB by eleven seconds. Every second counts, right? I placed 2,397[th] out of a field of starters of around 38,000, which put me in the top 6 per cent. I am still happy with that.

I cannot yet call myself a sub-three-hour marathon runner, but I am determined to get there one day. My performance in London means that I can qualify for Boston, London, and Berlin, so I have a couple of other races to choose from to try to better myself.

Post-race my cough was rather bad, and in hindsight I probably shouldn't have run that day, but fellow runners out there will understand the plight I was faced with when I woke up that morning.

So there we are. The Olympic challenge is truly over now, and it's time to take stock of the whole thing.

I loved every minute of it. Thanks to everyone who was a part of it.

Summer Modern Olympic Games Chronology

1896 – Athens
1900 – Paris
1904 – St. Louis
1908 – London
1912 – Stockholm
1916 – Berlin
1920 – Antwerp
1924 – Paris
1928 – Amsterdam
1932 – Los Angeles
1936 – Berlin
1948 – London
1952 – Helsinki
1956 – Melbourne
1960 - Rome

1964 – Tokyo
1968 – Mexico City
1972 – Munich
1976 – Montreal
1980 – Moscow
1984 – Los Angeles
1988 – Seoul
1992 – Barcelona
1996 – Atlanta
2000 – Sydney
2004 – Athens
2008 – Beijing
2012 – London
2016 – Rio De Janeiro

My Olympic Tour Dates

Athens – Marathon (October 2010)

London – London Marathon (2016), Moonwalk (May 2008 and May 2012), Step Change (March 2011), Great Drag Race (June 2011 and 2012), Ealing Half Marathon (September 2012 and 2013), Santa Dash (December 2012), Onesie Dash (March 2013), Tough Mudder (June 2013), Streak for Tigers (August 2013)

Tokyo – Five-kilometre time trial (August 2012)

Stockholm – Half marathon (September 2012)

Helsinki – Half marathon (September 2012)

Istanbul – Fifteen-kilometre race (November 2012)

Barcelona – Half marathon (February 2013)

Rome – Ten-kilometre sightseeing run (February 2013)

Paris – Half marathon (February 2013)

Antwerp – Ten-mile race (April 2013)

Berlin – Twenty-five-kilometre race (May 2013)

Amsterdam – Two-kilometre city swim race (September 2013)

Beijing – Triathlon (September 2013)

Munich – Half marathon (October 2013)

Montreal – Hypothermic half marathon (February 2014)

Moscow – Seven-kilometre race (April 2014)

Sydney – Fourteen-kilometre City to Surf race (August 2014)

Melbourne – Half marathon (August 2014)

Seoul – Marathon (March 2015)

Los Angeles – Tinkerbell half marathon (May 2015)

Atlanta – Big Peach Running Shop run (October 2015)
St. Louis – Rock 'n' Roll half marathon (October 2015)
Mexico City – Hash House Harriers running club (November 2015)
Rio – Correa de Sebastio (January 2016)

The cast

Many people accompanied me at various points on this journey. I refer to some of them throughout the book but I thought it may help having a cast list for you to refer to in case I mention their name and you wonder who they are:

Steven – the boyfriend
Natalie – my sister
Jessica – my niece
Mum – she gave birth to me
Dad – he helped make me
Laura – BFF
Claire – lifelong friend from University
Sophie – originally a client of mine but now a good friend
Michelle – school friend who supported me in the Amsterdam race
Fiona – school friend who supported me in the Barcelona race
Katie – school friend who now lives in Rome and spent the day
    with me there
Heather – school friend who lives in Melbourne and ran with me
    there
Mark – Heather's other half who also ran with me in Melbourne
Karen – school friend who lives in Adelaide and ran in Sydney
    with me
Alan – Karen's other half who ran with us in Sydney
Lucy – school friend who now lives in Sydney and force fed me
    champagne there
Karen – Aussie friend who never fails to make me laugh

Acknowledgements

A book or long journey simply isn't complete without a thank you section. Many people have helped me complete this challenge and I genuinely want to say a hearty cheers to you all for listening to me talk about it and helping me get to the end. That goes out to all of my friends, family and colleagues. You have supported me more than you know.

You have travelled with me to races. Stood on the side lines of races. Allowed me to spend a great deal of time training. Helped build my training programmes. Taken part in races with me. Told me that I could do it. Had faith that I would complete the challenge.

Mum, Dad, Steven, Natalie, Jessica, Laura, Claire, Sophie, Fiona, Katie, Michelle, Karen Sloane, Karen O'Kane, Alan O'Kane, The Big Peach Running Shop, Sight Jogging Rome, Heather, Mark, Namban Runners, Hash House Harriers Mexico City, Sarah & James Thorpe, the Karlberg family, Susanne Ericson, Laura Turner, David Chalfen, and Wayne Harvey. You have all been present at one or more of the races on this journey (or helped me prepare for it or design the book cover) and I thank you for that.

Finally; thanks to you for taking the time to read this.

About the Author

The author has lived in Athens, Brussels, Perth (Scotland), Newcastle upon Tyne, Sydney, and London. He enjoys stories (in book, theatre, or film form), urban areas, and travel. He has travelled to over seventy-five countries (to date) and studied tourism at university, and he has worked in the industry ever since. Travelling was therefore always in his genetic make-up. Running wasn't. Entering his first half marathon at the age of twenty-six, he became an addict. He ran in races across the UK and the occasional one abroad. He enjoyed it and lost his beer belly. He then thought about racing in every Summer Olympics city. To his knowledge, nobody had done it before. He could then combine travel and his newfound love of running. To date, he has taken part in more than eighty-five races across six continents (spanning half and full marathons, ten kilometres, five kilometres, swims, and triathlons), making him a seasoned runner after less than ten of years after partaking in the sport.

About the Book

The author was lucky enough to be living and working in London during the 2012 Olympics. He was sad to see the end of the games and wondered how he could continue to keep the Olympics alive a little longer. Feeling a little dusty after a heavy night for the closing ceremony, he sat at work thinking. It didn't take long to come up with the plan to race in every host city of the Summer Olympics before the next Olympics began four years later. Could it be done? He'd certainly give it a shot.

Scouring the Internet to find marathons, half marathons, ten kilometres, triathlons, swim races, and running clubs in each of the twenty-three cities, he made a plan to ensure he covered the globe within the timeframe he set himself (along with not going over his annual leave allowance from work). During the following three and a half years, there was a lot of training, races were done (sometimes even won), falls were had, he got lost in Asia, there were photo shoots on Copacabana Beach, and personal records were broken. For anyone interested in sport, travel, or just enjoying a giggle at somebody's sometimes misfortunes, this may be the book for you.

Lightning Source UK Ltd.
Milton Keynes UK
UKOW05f1532150617
303390UK00001B/82/P

9 781524 662882